Africa
Beyond the Mirror

Africa Beyond the Mirror

Boubacar Boris Diop

Translated from the French by
Vera Wülfing-Leckie
and
Caroline Beschea-Fache

ayebia

An Adinkra symbol
meaning Ntesie matemasie
A symbol of knowledge and wisdom

For Annie Jouga and Vieux Savané

For Théogène Karabayinga and Seydou Nourou Ndiaye

When the memory goes out to collect dead wood,
it brings back any bundle it likes.

Birago Diop – after a Wolof proverb

First published in French as *L'Afrique Au-delà du Miroir* by Éditions Philippe Rey,
2007 in Paris, France.

This edition first published in English in the UK by
Ayebia Clarke Publishing Limited in 2014
Ayebia Clarke Publishing Limited
7 Syringa Walk
Banbury
Oxfordshire
OX16 1FR
UK
www.ayebia.co.uk

ISBN 978-0-9569307-5-0

Distributed outside Africa, Europe and the United Kingdom
and exclusively in the USA by
Lynne Rienner Publishers, Inc.
1800 30th Street, Ste. 314
Boulder, CO 80301
USA
www.rienner.com

Distributed in Africa, Europe and the UK by TURNAROUND Publisher Services
at www.turnaround-uk.com

British Library Cataloguing-in-Publication Data
Cover Design by Claire-Nalin Designs UK
Typeset by FiSH Books, Enfield, Middlesex, UK
Printed and bound by CPI Group (UK) Ltd, Croydon, CR0 4YY
Available from www.ayebia.co.uk or email info@ayebia.co.uk
Distributed in Europe, UK by TURNAROUND at www.turnaround-uk.com

Distributed in Southern Africa Jonathan Ball Publishers, Cape Town, South Africa
Website: www.jonathanball.co.za and Orders: orders@jonathanball.co.za

Also available from www.ayebia.co.uk or email info@ayebia.co.uk

Table of Contents

Preface

Boubacar Boris Diop: The Duty of Lucidity.

On September 26, 2002, Senegal was struck by the worst tragedy of its post-independence history: the sinking of the ferry *Le Joola* which claimed hundreds and hundreds of victims. It has been assessed that when the ferry capsized off the coast of Gambia on its way from the southern city of Ziguinchor to the capital, Dakar, it took with her more lives than were lost in the *Titanic*. The toll was particularly high among the women and the children on board. Many of the victims were students returning to their different schools in Dakar after having spent some vacation home, in the green land of the Casamance region. I knew a few of them who were my students at the Philosophy department of Cheikh Anta Diop University. I still recall the posters we put up on a board *in memoriam*. They were all smiles and confidence and happiness on those posters for which their university identification pictures had been used.

For weeks the disaster was lived in a state of shock by all. There was a need for many of us to put it in words that would give some meaning to what had happened and what we were going through. In the December issue of the French monthly *Le Monde Diplomatique*, a few weeks after the disaster, those words came at last, in an article entitled "A Letter to a Friend about the Sinking of the *Joola*" dated December 15, 2002. The "letter" expressed at once deep sorrow for the lives that had been lost, profound compassion for the mourners, many of them having been left without even the relative solace of having retrieved the bodies of their loved ones to bury. It also expressed the deep anger felt by many in the face of what was certainly not just "another African tragedy," of what could not possibly be considered "an inevitable accident." The article showed with the utmost precision all that the disaster had to tell about Senegalese policies and politics at the time. Every single word of it rang true and struck the right chord: Boubacar Boris Diop, its author, had been once again the voice attuned to the African experience.

"A Letter to a Friend about the Sinking of the *Joola*" is one of the articles, contributions and lectures by Senegalese writer Boubacar Boris Diop gathered here. They take us beyond the mirror, on the other side of the usual image of Africa presented by the media. As B.B. Diop writes, "the image of Africa, portrayed in specialized media and other works, is not pretty. It does not depict reality in any way, despite what some of us may say in desperation, out of intellectual dishonesty, or out of spinelessness."(p. 3). The virtue he cultivates, both as a novelist and journalist, is certainly the absolute opposite of desperation, dishonesty and spinelessness: to express it in one single word, it is lucidity. Boubacar Boris Diop's struggle for Africa is at the same time passionate love for the continent and the most demanding lucidity about what the multifarious African experience is and means.

It is not that Boris (as his friends call him) claims for himself or for the corporation of writers a particular privilege of lucidity. On the contrary, it is because he blames himself for having fallen into the trap of self-identification with the Africa presented in the mirror of the media that he has assigned to his writing the task, indeed the duty, of lucidity. When he is asked in interviews to comment about the special "eye" with which he has examined the Rwandan Genocide in his novel *Murambi: The Book of Bones*[1], B. B. Diop always recalls that in his previous novel, *Le cavalier et son ombre*, he had been so careless that he had even painted killers (those who fled to the Kivu region when they were chased by the Rwandan army of the Patriotic Liberation front led by Kagame) as heroes. When he then explains how he could have been thus misled, here is what Boris has to say: "the international press greatly contributed to that confusion but I do not want to hold it responsible for my own unawareness, which would be a little bit too easy. If I could have so easily mistaken the killers for their victims, it is mainly because of the image of Africa I had formed. I had come to internalize the widespread idea that Africa is the continent where ragged people kill one another all the time with a ferocity that defies any rational analysis. One cannot imagine how much self-contempt it takes to adopt those racist prejudices in one's novels or plays, pleading sometimes that it is humour. It allows one to pass for somebody courageous and lucid..."[2] True lucidity is what is required, for Diop, from one who takes the responsibility to write. The demand for the lucidity that takes the writer and the reader beyond the appearance in the mirror is the commanding principle of Boris' writing. And nowhere is that lucidity more manifest than in his novels, especially *Murambi: The Book of Bones.*

Comparing the writing of the historian and that of the novelist, B.B. Diop explains here why the truth is on the side of the latter: "Can the serenity of a historian depict this outburst of the wildest human passions? I don't think so. The novel, which meets the killer on his own ground of emotion and falsification, seems more suitable to fulfill this task." (p. 16) Those words are written in the first of the three essays that make up the first part of the book. That part is devoted to the Genocide of the Tutsis in Rwanda in 1994. Diop's statement explains why it can be said that *Murambi*, though a work of fiction, is today one of the very best testimonies about what happened in 1994 in Rwanda. In many interviews and lectures, the author often insists that the writing of *Murambi* had to be, and indeed has been, a break away from his previous works, from the style he had adopted until then and which he had come to see as indulging too often in some hocus-pocus associated with the kind of experimental writing that used to be his trademark.[3] Those who are familiar with Diop's work will certainly disagree with this harsh judgment about himself but they will also perceive in it the driving force behind his oeuvre: the demand for sincerity, for lucidity.

The three essays collected here on the Rwandan tragedy raise crucial questions about what Toni Morrison has written, a propos *Murambi*, about the capacity of art to restore meaning after a genocide. They explore and denounce the more or less passive complicities that made it possible for the killers to perpetrate their crimes. The other disquisitions in this book are also important contributions to major issues that confront Africa today. Thus, Diop interrogates the meaning of globalization from the perspective of "The New Wretched of the Earth," that is the young Africans risking their lives to emigrate to Europe or to "the New World;" he also explores the future of African literature in indigenous African languages or evaluates the legacy of Cheikh Anta Diop, for whom he has the greatest admiration. All manifest what is the commanding principle of Boubacar Boris Diop's writing: the demand for the lucidity necessary to get beyond the image in the mirror of an invented Africa.

Souleymane Bachir Diagne,
Columbia University

Introduction

In the past, the publication of a work of fiction used to mean that its author could say 'Mission Accomplished.' Now, it seems that this is only where it all starts: there are so many talks, book fairs and festivals, that it has become very difficult to escape the ritual of public readings. *Prima facie*, what could be more bonding than the interaction between dozens, even hundreds of people and the poet *reciting* his or her own opus on stage? And yet, one cannot help feeling taken aback that these days, not only the creation, but also the promotion of a text seems to rest firmly on the shoulders of the writer. The hypothetical audiences to whom these narratives are addressed no longer see the need to make the effort to familiarize themselves with them on their own. Instead, they have the cheek to say: "Have you finished writing your book? Well then, what are you waiting for? Read it to me!"

That must be the reason why so many novelists, the new globetrotters, never stop hopping from continent to continent to attend these rather strange *tête-à-têtes* with women and men they will maybe only see once and never again. It seems as though ultimately, a lot depends on these meetings with the public in all four corners of the world. The writer is constantly expected to justify his or her narrative choices and to react in a suitably contrite manner to the calamities afflicting mankind.

Obviously, one tries to make a good impression, but the exercise is both delicate and ambiguous. Due to his eloquence, the author may come across as a superficial extrovert, or worse still, he may end up distracting attention from the seminal works in question.

On the other hand, these live encounters do have certain advantages. They suggest, quite unexpectedly, that orality may be superior to the written word after all, by establishing a much stronger bond between the writer and his audience than before. Instead of dealing with a purely abstract concept, the author meets his readers in the flesh and knows their faces and their expectations. He might even go so far as to claim he feels haunted by them night and day. Furthermore, the shock of meeting the elusive reader gradually creates a sense of urgency and the need to articulate one's views on political issues, which are often extremely difficult to disentangle.

While everyone ought to take a stance, the African intellectual is morally obliged to speak up, particularly if he has even the slightest chance of being heard.

Between 1992 and 2006, my desire to do just that led to the publication of numerous essays in different journals, while others were written at the special request of universities. They make up the bulk of this book, but not without having been carefully revised in certain instances. It may have been necessary to bring the statistical data up to date, or to add new facts. Some of the articles had not yet been properly edited in their unabridged form as in the case of the "Letter to a Friend about the Sinking of the Joola," and also "Kigali-Paris: The Two-Headed Monster", both of which had been shortened on the occasion of a previous publication – in the latter case under a different title – due to the space constraints in both the French monthly *Le Monde Diplomatique* and the Senegalese journal *Le Quotidien.*

Besides articles paying homage to Cheikh Anta Diop and Mongo Beti, others deal with subjects as diverse as the dilemma of the writer who is caught between two languages, a ferry disaster in Senegal, a new migratory tide moving towards Europe, or the cultural challenges of globalization. What they all have in common, though, is that they endeavour to examine what it really means to be African by trying to find out whether this is just a politically correct red herring, or a true reflection of our daily lives. The picture the media and books by supposedly well-informed authors paint of Africa is not pretty. But what is so upsetting is that it has nothing whatsoever to do with reality no matter what some of us may say, either out of desperation or intellectual dishonesty or simple cowardice. When reading and listening to the utterances of racists – and a number of them are clearly not aware that that is what they are – one occasionally has the impression that the world has never been so peaceful, that the heads of government of all the nations on earth are just and pure and that our continent is the only one where corruption and poverty are rampant. They all seem oblivious of the planks in their own eye while lecturing others about the splinters in theirs. If I decided to visit Baghdad or Kabul right now, I presume that, between two staggering bloodbaths, people would find the time to express their consternation about the ravages of political violence and the famines in Africa. Where exactly "in Africa"? In Dakar? In Nairobi? The question stares us in the face, but is seldom asked: for some reason it seems that most people, as soon as they set foot on African soil, imagine themselves to be in the whole of Africa at the same time. No matter that the Democratic Republic of Congo alone is bigger than all of Western Europe. The suggestion that the inhabitants of such a vast continent are all one and the same is so utterly absurd that one simply doesn't know what to say. The thinking behind this is of course not as naïve as it seems, but born out of the desire to make black people ashamed of their history and their identity. That is unacceptable.

It is not hard to guess why I have devoted so much space to the Genocide of the Tutsis in Rwanda.

There are still commentators with questionable motives trying to convince us that basically nothing happened in Rwanda between April and July 1994. Such hypocrisy must not be allowed to persist.

I have stressed the involvement of France in the genocide because its responsibility under François Mitterrand was as obvious as it is poorly known or accepted and yet, we have more than enough evidence to support this. Equally, it is no coincidence that in France, revisionism has been allowed to proliferate so openly and unchecked that it takes one's breath away. It may be unrealistic to expect people who try to play down the seriousness of the Slave Trade and make pronouncements on the benefits of colonization to recognize that their country was a forceful and determined accomplice in the last genocide of the 20th century; but to remind them of this at every opportunity is a necessary exercise in intellectual hygiene.

It is all the more important to place the Rwandan tragedy at the centre of these reflections since it serves as an excellent illustration of outside interference intended to prove how violent and full of fratricidal hatred African culture really is. To suggest that the genocide of 1994 is behind us, is basically saying that several hundred thousands of Rwandan Tutsis deserved to die under the most abominable conditions and that we must stop making such a song and dance about it. To remain silent on this subject would be tantamount to giving free rein to a kind of anti-black racism that has lost all sense of shame. But cast your eye beyond the mirror and you are trying to expose the extremely serious counter–truths which are hidden under all those stereotypes. Above all, it means setting off alarm bells, since the sinister political strategy behind this arrogant negrophobia is very clear.

Two essays – "Senegal Between Cheikh Anta Diop and Senghor" and "Transforming Genocide into Art" – are based on lectures I gave at Austin University in Texas and at Brandeis in Boston (Massachusetts); "Carona, the Global Village," owes its existence to a grant I received from ProHelvetia, the Swiss cultural foundation. I am grateful to all of them for giving me the opportunity to write about these very important subjects. Most of the texts that are assembled in this book, however, were composed at the request of the *Neue Zürcher Zeitung.* I would like to give special thanks to this German language daily paper in Zürich for having allowed me, on so many occasions over the past twenty-one years, to freely express my opinion on the interesting issues of our time. I owe the same gratitude to all the other newspapers with which I have had the privilege of working more or less regularly during the same period. Apart from *Le Monde Diplomatique* and *Le Quotidien,* which I have mentioned before, I am referring to two weeklies, the *Internazionale* and *Courrier International,* published in Italy and France respectively.

SECTION I

Rwanda: Against the Habit of Misery

Transforming Genocide into Art

In the course of the past ten years, the number of people who have heard of Rwanda has grown by leaps and bounds and that includes many who never used to have the slightest interest in the African continent. The reason for this is well known, but it is sad indeed that this tiny country with no natural resources should have had to go through so much more than its fair share of suffering to attract all this attention.

The speed with which the international community has taken cognisance of the Rwandan Genocide – without making any attempt to avert it – was only matched by the speed with which it was executed. According to the UN, the massacres which took place from April to July 1994 resulted in the deaths of between 500,000 and 800,000 people.[4] The Rwandan authorities have still not disclosed the final tally of victims, but the figure has been estimated to be in excess of one million, which seems perfectly credible.

In order to understand what happened in Rwanda, one has to imagine 10,000 people being killed there *every single day*, for three months, without interruption.

This extermination was not some hare-brained undertaking that was launched on the spur of the moment, due to unforeseeable political circumstances. Far from it – it had been very carefully planned. A strongly centralized state had made its army, its paramilitary forces[5] – created specifically for that purpose – and its entire administration available for the purpose of the elimination of a part of the Rwandan population, selected on the grounds of its 'ethnicity'.

At the time, almost none of the commentators seemed to comprehend the gravity of the situation. Most of them saw in this genocide a new style of 'inter-ethnic massacre', a kind of travesty of a 'civil war', where two population groups that have hated each other since time immemorial, clash. The repeated use of these terms eventually convinced the entire world that in April 1994, Rwanda was not divided into executioners and victims, that the Rwandan government, completely taken by surprise by the events, was doing its best to re-establish law and order in the country and finally, that this anarchy, these atrocities in the tropics, eluded any sort of rational political analysis. This last idea, which partly explains the passivity of the United Nations, had been reinforced by the manner in which the continent was portrayed in the media.

It would of course be absurd to suggest that the international press conspired to make things easier for the killers. It had no reason whatsoever to behave vindictively against Rwanda. The truth is at the same time much less complicated and more depressing: nobody was really very interested in Rwanda.

If it is a fact that basically any Western country involved in this conflict could easily find reliable contacts among the special envoys and media correspondents to help them spread disinformation, then many of the latter have mainly sinned through their indifference and by listening only to their prejudices. Since Africa is widely perceived to be the natural birthplace of every catastrophe, the massacres in Rwanda were only just another tragedy long after – or at the same time as – those that took place in Somalia, Algeria and Liberia. If one isn't allowed to call that racism, it is because these words have lost their meaning.

This explains why the Rwandan Genocide still holds such a singular status, even today. Hardly anyone has the audacity to deny the blindingly obvious fact that it happened. However, when it comes to identifying the perpetrators and bringing them to justice, serious difficulties arise. It has become the norm to associate the great infamies of our recent history with specific individuals in order to anchor them forever in our memory: the names of Hitler and Pol Pot, examples of monstrous 'Masters of the Universe', usurpers of the power over life and death, instantly bring to mind gas chambers and killing fields. But the Rwandan Genocide has remained nameless, since that would have necessitated a choice between Good and Evil. And it looks as though, in this particular case, the compassion for the victims stops short of the recognition of their innocence.

Having said this, one has to be honest and admit that the Rwandan tragedy has aroused almost less interest in Africa itself than in the rest of the world.

The paradox is obvious. Both Cheikh Anta Diop and Kwame Nkrumah repeatedly voiced their concerns over the way the African continent had been carved up into barely viable states; the long-term effect of this is that today, we are often faced with completely unexpected situations. One such example is the fact that Africa gets its information about its own political problems from the countries of the North. Strange as it may seem, but everything many francophone Africans knew about the Rwandan Genocide came from the dispatches of *Agence France-Presse,* the major French daily papers and the television news programmes by Messrs. Poivre d'Arvor and Masure. The African private press was not very developed during the 1990s and lacked the means to counter this trend. It was simply not in a position to send journalists into the field to get another angle on the conflict. What's worse is that one cannot even be sure that the African media, had they been there, would have steered clear of the usual clichés about the chaos on this continent. By dint of its failures, Africa has lost all self-respect. And whatever happens here, our distinguished analysts will be the first to explain this as Africa's alleged inability to adapt to the modern world, maybe due – to make things even more distressing – to some ancient curse.

It is sad but true that, among the rare cries of indignation that were heard during the genocide, almost none came from Africa. Nelson Mandela, who had just been elected as the new head of government in post-Apartheid South Africa, was a laudable exception. We may have quietly expressed our disgust on a few occasions, but otherwise, there was almost total indifference.

So the project 'Rwanda: Writing against Oblivion' [Rwanda: écrire par devoir de mémoire] came about as a reaction to the 'deafening silence' from African intellectuals and artists.

It all started in 1995, during the fifth annual convention of Fest'Africa.[6] On November 10 of that year, the meeting was overshadowed by the news of the death sentence and subsequent hanging at Port Harcourt of the Nigerian writer and activist Ken Saro-Wiwa and eight of his co-detainees. The authors present at Fest'Africa decided there and then to express their outrage in a public declaration against the military dictatorship of Sani Abacha.

It was not the first time that Men of Letters had voiced feelings of frustration at their inability to stay the hands of criminal heads of state.

After several months, this bitter statement had intensified in us the need to be heard. Discussions with the Rwandan community in Paris clearly showed the need to take a greater interest in the genocide of 1994. Then came the suggestion that a number of authors from different African countries should travel to Rwanda and spend some time there as writers in residence.

However, things were not as straightforward as we had thought. It took nothing less than three years to convince the initially reticent Rwandan authorities to let us into their country. Clearly, the arrival of a group of mostly francophone writers for a project financed by the 'Foundation of France' was hardly reassuring for them. Their reserve was quite understandable, in fact, since it had been partly in defence of the French language that Mitterrand and the *Françafrique* network had so unscrupulously decided to back the organizers of the genocide. Nocky Djedanoum eventually succeeded in persuading the Kigali officials with words that were both polite and firm: "As an African I demand the right to go wherever I want in Rwanda and you have no choice but to give your permission." After the necessary briefings, everything then fell into place.

Our group stayed in Rwanda during July and August of 1998[7] and we used the opportunity to visit the Genocide Memorial, to talk to NGOs such as Lawyers without Borders [*Avocats sans Frontières*] and the co-operative Pro'Femmes and to meet the Journalists and Writers Association of Rwanda, as well as the directors of the Polyclinic of Hope, one of the organizations which care for children who were orphaned and women who were raped during the genocide. In addition to this, we gave lectures at the university of Butare and in secondary and primary schools. And of course we had meetings with the survivors – including those who are now members of Ibuka[8] – as well as with some of the one hundred and twenty thousand prisoners accused of having participated in the massacres in various different ways. A lot of time was deliberately kept free so it could be used for the actual compilation of our notes and for individual projects.

Nine out of the ten texts that were originally planned have been published so far, and the last (*Great Sadness,* by Meja Mwangi) should be ready for publication soon. Our books were first presented to the Rwandan public in June 2000 during an international symposium in Kigali and Butare. The dramatist Koulsy Lamko had selected passages from each of these texts and combined them into an excellent show with the title *Bodies and Voices, Rhizome Words* [Corps et voix, paroles rhizomes].

While all this was going on, we started seeing new initiatives in various fields of the Arts, inspired by our project. Examples of this are the Cameroonian movie director François Wokouache who decided to join and made a 124-minute film with the title *We Are No Longer Dead* about the project, while another filmmaker, Samba Félix Ndiaye from Senegal, produced an ambitious documentary about the same subject, called *Rwanda, Against*

Oblivion, [Rwanda, pour mémoire]. Then there is the South African artist Bruce Clarke who is planning to construct a gigantic stone monument on the hill at Nyanza. It will be dedicated to the victims and will be called *The Garden of Memory*. Two choreographers – Germaine Acogny from Senegal and Kota Yamasaki from Japan – have produced *Fagaala,*[9] which is based on *Murambi: The Book of Bones.*

Since March 2000, when our texts first became available to the public, they have not only been translated into several languages, but they have also attracted a lot of media attention at literary events, both in Africa and Europe. The November 2000 Book Fair in Lille was especially dedicated to works associated with 'Rwanda: Writing against Oblivion.'

Clearly, such an initiative brings with it a certain number of problems that I am by no means trying to hide.

The first one of these is related to the actual process itself. Several writers had travelled to the scene of a tragedy *together,* with each one *independently* planning to write a work of fiction about this tragedy. This in itself must be quite unique in the history of literature. But writing is by its very nature an exquisitely solitary act. The literary text, it seems, somehow takes shape in retrospect, as a result of largely subconscious mechanisms. Paradoxically, the novelist himself tends to be unaware of this; he likes to think he is firmly in control of what happens in the book, from beginning to end. That is why being commissioned to write can be so difficult. One somehow feels hampered in one's creative freedom, the very thing which usually motivates the choice to become a writer in the first place.

While this must have been why we responded so enthusiastically to the idea of going to Rwanda, we did so with a vague sense of apprehension. I remember, for instance, having replied to Nocky Djedanoum that I wanted to go to Rwanda and bring back a sort of travel journal. I was convinced that the best I could do was to describe everything with an icy neutrality: the mutual killings between Hutu and Tutsi, the tranquil sky above the hills, the fruit sellers by the side of the road, in short, the way life was getting back to normal in anticipation of the killings between Hutus and Tutsis starting afresh. Looking back today, it is easy for me to see my attitude at the time as a kind of insecurity. I did not think that I would have very much to say about a topic which for me at the time, was essentially an example of the deplorable excesses of tribal barbarism, no doubt about it and one had seen it all before. And since I was so used to forging the plots of my novels exactly as I pleased and being proud of it, I felt ill at ease in a situation where the brutal facts, with all their power, predated the fictionalized account.

In other words, I had trouble getting used to the idea that my imagination would be curbed by life itself. We all knew in advance that the most basic respect for the victims forbade taking too many liberties with their eyewitness accounts. It is worth mentioning, by the way, the desperate pleas made by some of the survivors, from the moment they understood the purpose of our visit to Rwanda: "We implore you not to write things in your novel which didn't actually happen to us; you must repeat faithfully what we have told you. The entire world has to find out exactly what went on here." It should also be pointed out that we had an understanding with the organizers that it was entirely up to each of us whether we wanted to write anything at all. Despite that, nine of the ten books that had been planned at the outset are available now. At the end of the day, one might say the survivors and the dead silently commissioned us to write these texts. I will try to explain later how easy it was for them to make us abandon our little artistic vanities.

Then there was the risk that the encounter with such an utterly unspeakable reality might make one lose all desire to write anything ever again. The Zimbabwean novelist Chenjerai Hove was contacted and asked to join our group, but, after much deliberation, he declined the offer. This is how he explained his decision in Lille, in November 2000: "I was afraid of being so traumatized that I would no longer be able to write fiction." It is true that breaking through the mirror – a piece of glass in which so many of our failures and blunders are reflected – rather than making us masters of our destiny, can lead to madness and despair.

Finally, one might ask how useful such an intervention, four years after the genocide, can possibly be. The Rwandan schoolchildren were saying just that when they asked the question, again and again and with more bitterness than rage: "Why have you only come now? Where were you four years ago, when all this was happening in our country?"

These objections are serious and can be very disturbing. Nevertheless, these obstacles not only didn't bother us, they actually spurred us on. And although it was a collective adventure, each one of us delved into it with his own priorities and itinerary in mind. This tension, born out of the clash between reality and imagination, was a novel experience for all of us. What was so special about it was the fact that it helped us rediscover emotions with a new authenticity. Coming into contact with the most profound pain made us raise our voices against the pernicious power of prejudice and at the same time re-evaluate our responsibilities as intellectuals.

Why was it really necessary for us to go to Rwanda in order to experience the madness of the times we live in? We know, after all, that in Africa, just as in many other places on this planet, a writer's desk is never far away from a mass grave somewhere. Fanaticism kills people *en masse* both in the air and on the ground and the media talk about it all the time. Is it therefore not a stupid excuse to pretend, in the case of Rwanda for instance, that we didn't know? I can only respond to these questions by giving the example I know best, which is my own. Before this novel about the genocide, I published another one, *The Horseman and his Shadow,* [Le Cavalier et son ombre],[10] in which Rwanda plays a very important role. But I had never been to Rwanda and I frankly had certain doubts as to whether my feelings were genuine. And that is why the only moment in the story when Khadidja, the heroine, is really speaking with the author's voice, is when she is talking about the anguish she feels about the genocide, mixed with a secret resentment of her own wrath, as though it were all just some sort of melodrama.

Due to the sheer ignorance of the writer, the tragedies told in this novel take place in Mugunga and Uvira, two camps Khadidja specifically names in the book. These camps, like some of the others, were full of innocent refugees, but the majority of the organisers and perpetrators of the genocide were there too. They had been taken there by the supposedly humanitarian *Opération Turquoise,* and then continued to rule the camps. In the novel, Khadidja, the narrator, talks about these killers with a lot of sympathy and feeling: she describes, for example, how they are taking care of the most vulnerable people in the camp. This is reminiscent of a fictional story about the Gestapo in Lyon during the Occupation, in which the French author turns Klaus Barbie into the protector of a widow and an orphan. This analogy is not meant as a sort of self-flagellation. It just seems useful to me to demonstrate how easily social chaos manifests itself through an identical disorder in the heads of the most dubious members of society. The creators of this chaos are so much more vulnerable than they are prepared to admit, and, just like Khadidja, they perceive the victims and their executioners as an amorphous block, without making a distinction between the causes and the consequences of what is happening. This tendency to react to all political calamities whose only common denominator is that they have occurred in Africa, with a sort of universal lamentation, opens the floodgates to all the most abominable clichés. Specific situations and *a fortiori,* individual human beings, start to look blurred. It's not about what is going on in Liberia, Somalia or the Congo, but what is going on in Africa. Similarly, this genocide didn't take place in a country called Rwanda, but just "in Africa:" the writer sheds some tears over the victims of the dictator, then portrays the latter in the worst possible light in order to get the audience on his side and hey presto, he can move on with his conscience intact.

When we went to Rwanda, reality was in our face. I myself experienced much more extreme emotions than Khadidja, the narrator, in *The Horseman and his Shadow*. The fact that Khadidja claims to 'feel Rwanda's pain' is of course nonsense. It's the others who had to bear all that suffering. The author, very far removed from their pain and simply keen to *mimic reality* through a thousand and one stylistic shenanigans, had really just been inflicting aesthetic torture upon himself. It had given me a great deal of satisfaction to play around with real events and to freeze fickle and ephemeral forms with words. It was a purely literary pursuit. I think this qualifies me to explain the difference between a novel about genocide, penned at a safe distance, in the comfort of our daily routine and another, written with the stench of death in our nostrils. In the first case, the temptation to use shocking images is very great, since in Africa, reality can be so mind-blowingly cruel that the competition with fiction simply seems unfair. The African novelist, who is well aware of this, often has no choice but to embellish his story with fantastical details if he wants to keep up the pace. This on-going fictional contest is exhausting, even for the most talented artist. At the same time, he is putting the credibility of his story on the line. Before I went to Rwanda, I felt no need whatsoever to stick to the facts. I found it difficult to comprehend those for whom writing is all about telling the truth. I used to find it much more exciting to stir up doubts and uncertainty. The writer was for me a bit like a lost child in the forest and I used to delight in the solitude so aptly described by the poet Birago Diop who said: 'when the memory goes out to collect dead wood, it brings back any bundle it likes'.[11] We should pause here for a moment and imagine the perplexity of someone who is in the middle of a forest, trying to 'collect dead wood.' He wanders from one bush to the next, frequently retracing his steps, constantly wondering – with great anxiety – which direction he should take and he never seems to know what he is doing or why he is doing it. All he really wants, in the end, is to confess that he does not know the way, that he cannot show it to anyone, that he does not know where he is going and that he cannot walk there in a straight line.

This desire to write, not with ideas, but with memories, or rather with echoes of words from deep inside, from dark and far-away places, could be perceived as a little bit conceited. Going to Rwanda helped me understand that what I would find there was despair in abundance and an almost ineffable sense of my own impotence.

Stepping over human remains as we were talking to the survivors made us at the same time more humble and more conscious of what our books might be able to achieve in the fight against evil. It was only gradually that the full extent of the Rwandan tragedy and its human implications became clear to us. Each testimony was given in an atmosphere of absolute terror. The killing of so many people in just a few weeks means that hundreds of thousands of killers were working in broad daylight and not all of them have been arrested, far from it. It also means that on the hills or in the streets of Kigali, of Butare or Gitarama, the paths of the executioners and the victims are continuing to cross. They recognize each other; they know who they are; they have blood-curdling images awakened from a recent past dancing in their memories. And they continue on their way, since despite everything, life must go on.

It did not take us long to realize that the only way we could hope to heal such profound distress was to pledge ourselves to simplicity. During readings of the books we had written about the genocide, it was immediately obvious that apart from the differences in approach and personality, they were all similar in terms of their austerity of style and a certain reserve. What sort of writers would we be, had we returned home from Rwanda, full of ourselves and eager to show off our narrative acrobatics and perfectly crafted metaphors?

Since their publication from March 2000 onwards, we have often been asked what our books have achieved that had not already been achieved by all the newspaper articles, documentaries, historical tomes and victims' eyewitness accounts.

This question is of enormous importance, since it opens up the debate about the effectiveness of fiction in the battle against oblivion. Our particular literary context makes this question even more pertinent. The African author is more susceptible to feelings of doubt and discouragement than practically anybody else. Writing in a foreign language for an audience far too preoccupied with survival to be interested in his books tends to make him feel utterly alone – howling his rebellion into the desert. The violence of the civil wars on this continent assaults him with questions that require immediate answers, placing his work, which often strikes him as delicate, vain and of uncertain value, under the relentless pressure of political emergencies.

But that is also the very reason why these novels play such an important role in keeping the memory of this genocide alive. Academic dissertations, with all their precision, hold less attraction for the public at large since they are less accessible. They are aimed at an intellectual elite expected to analyze them without much emotional involvement. And then, everyone knows the little quip that experts don't read each other so much as *they survey each other.* Similarly to the journalist, who is beholden to deadlines and forced, so to speak, to jump from one massacre to the next, the historian has no choice but to let the dead bury the dead. The novelist, on the other hand, tries to bring them back to life and this desire to play God can become an obsession. I remember that in Rwanda, every time we went to visit places where there are still skeletons and bones of victims openly exposed, I felt the need to look for even the tiniest signs of life around us, just as one would open a window very slightly to let a little bit of fresh air into a place which is otherwise completely hermetically sealed. One of these episodes is briefly described in *Murambi: The Book of Bones.* It was only later that I was able to make sense of my behaviour. The truth is that a toy next to the crushed skull of a child says so much more about the genocide than the most learned presentations. What is important here is to show actual faces, not to report facts or roll out cold statistics. While the delirious cruelty of the perpetrators of this genocide is difficult to comprehend, it is not as senseless as one might think. By humiliating these innocent people before cutting them up with a machete, the killers wanted to convince themselves and especially their victims that they were not really human and that nature had erred by putting them on this earth. That may be why the denialists are always slightly taken aback when one holds up the evidence of facts and figures for them to see. In their view, nobody died, because the people we are making such a fuss about never had the right to exist in the first place. This is why writing fiction is an excellent way of opposing the *genocidaire* and his machinations. It gives the victims a soul, and, even if it does not resuscitate them, it at least gives them back their humanity through the ritual of mourning. The novel becomes a funerary stele. Written on it are the very simple words: Here lies.... They sum up what all our novels are about.

After the holocaust, many Germans were able to say, seemingly in good faith, that they did not know. Even this lie was not possible in Rwanda. The Rwandan Genocide was unusual in that the State succeeded in getting almost the entire population embroiled in it. It took place amid noise and fury, while hundreds of thousands of bodies were rotting on the hills, with a radio channel joyously co-ordinating the massacres and cries of hate mingling with screams of terror everywhere. Can the historian in his ivory tower give a fair description of what goes on when the most insane human instincts are unleashed? I don't think so. The novel, itself so familiar with emotions and falsifications, meets the killer on his own ground and thus seems to me a more suitable tool to fulfill this task. It is perhaps still the best way of rousing the ordinary man-in-the-street from his torpor as he watches his fellow-men being butchered all around him and throws up his arms, saying he is sincerely sorry but there are simply not enough hours in the day to do anything about it. While he is clearly not a killer himself, he doesn't realize that through his mental inertia he is aiding and abetting the scheming of fanatics ready to exterminate entire populations.

In the case of the decent ordinary family man dozing on his sofa, the novel is either going to pass him by, or it might awaken in him the desire to re-humanize himself.

Besides that, one is all the more entitled to write an imaginary account of the genocide since the recent history of Rwanda was largely the result of a conflict between truth and fiction. All these nightmarish delusions developed out of a certain colonial ethnology, which *fabricated* a non-African history in an African country and passed it off as science.

Colonial ethnology only came to Rwanda at the end of the 19th century, which was very late. However, it was quick in labelling its inhabitants according to racial criteria based on ideas prevalent in the West during that time. This ethnology considers the Hutu, who are of Bantu origin, as indigenous, just like the Twa – who are pygmies. These are the two negroid population groups: generally short, dark-skinned and supposedly mentally obtuse. The Tutsi, on the other hand, are showered with compliments about their fine facial features, light skin, pleasant nature, superior intelligence and above all their innate leadership abilities. The ethnologists were therefore not surprised that this minority managed to dominate the other two groups without any difficulty. The Tutsis were from then on portrayed as a Hamitic people who came from Egypt, via the Nile. Gradually, the entirely fatuous belief started to take hold that they were originally from Ethiopia. They have also been turned into Caucasians or Jews, to say nothing about other, even more far-fetched theories.

In short, it basically comes down to elaborate hypotheses which claim that the Tutsis are 'perhaps' a white population group in terms of their race, which might have gone astray deep in the interior of the Great Lakes region a very long time ago. The Belgian administrators were taking all this very seriously, claiming the Tutsis were 'genetically superior' and backing up these claims with anthropometric measurements and investigations into genes and blood groups. All these pseudo-scientific data were brought into play for the introduction of the infamous ethnic identity cards, which effectively allowed the majority of the potential victims to be identified in 1994. Although ethnicity in the strict sense of the word never used to be an issue in Rwanda, this colonial ethnology, when it became the dominant ideology, made the Rwandan people see themselves as racially completely different from each other. The Tutsis ended up paying a particularly terrible price for the notion that they were essentially foreigners: In Kabaya on November 22, 1992, when Leon Mugesera, one of the prominent Hutu extremist leaders was trying to justify the looming genocide, he quite naturally addressed the Tutsis in the following terms: "Your native country is Ethiopia and [...] we will shortly hasten your return home via the Nyabarongo River by special delivery." The tens of thousands of bodies seen floating on the Nyabarongo during the genocide were for the killers just a way of expediting the Tutsis' 'return home'.

And when in 1994, Bernard Kouchner told Mitterrand about his concerns regarding the crimes committed by the interim government with its close ties to Paris, the President of France bluntly put his mind at rest by saying: "This is a fight between master and servant!", the former being the Tutsis, of course.

So our group of writers went to Rwanda and we found a country that had something surreal about it. But our time there was not wasted.

The project 'Rwanda: Writing Against Oblivion' has come to play an important role in preserving what needs to be remembered about the genocide. These texts have sparked a number of discussions already and that will continue all over the world. That is proof, by the way, that different forms of expression are not necessarily opposed to each other. It is often in response to our novels that journalists return to the subject, sometimes to revise their original opinion.

We have made extensive use of history books and certain articles from the press in formulating our 'lies', which at the end of the day actually represent a deeper truth.

Is it not intriguing to picture a bunch of about ten writers turning up in a war-torn country, wandering around among ruins and broken bones, pen in hand and full of excitement? It is easy to see how pleased they are with themselves. This immense human tragedy is just the sort of subject they have been waiting for; it's serious and couldn't be more different from their usual shallow nonsense about the conflict between tradition and progress in Africa.

This freeze frame shot may be a deliberate and rather unfair parody, but it instantly put us at the centre of the debate. It was one of the rare occasions where the novelist's imagination is truly confronted with reality. But even more important was undoubtedly the confrontation of each one of us with himself. It is easy to comprehend that so much suffering cannot just dissolve into thin air overnight. Besides the duty to commemorate it, this journey to the outer edge of horror has also taught us an unforgettable history lesson.

Of course we have asked the same question over and over again: *why?* The people we engaged in conversation in Rwanda often admitted that they did not know the answer. And yet, there was no shortage of explanations. They spoke to us about a long tradition of total submission to the royal overlord, about the pernicious effect of ancient resentments and about Christianization gone wrong, – or, on the contrary, gone dramatically right? – thus depriving an old civilization of its points of reference even before the arrival of the foreigner, very late in the day at the end of the 19th century. We understood very quickly that it was imperative to hark back to that moment in time if we really wanted to find any helpful clues. Even if we had little chance of unravelling the whole conundrum, there was simply no way round the fact that such an extreme example of political violence as the one which took place in Rwanda, must have had its origin in colonialism. The Belgians may not have been directly involved in what happened in 1994, but historically, these events were the long-term effect of their political control of Rwanda and especially their utterly unreasonable decision to introduce ethnicity into the process of independence. The eruption of anti-Tutsi violence, which started in 1959, has sometimes been presented as a legitimate reaction to several centuries of feudal oppression. One would like to agree, but at this point, a quick glance at South Africa is essential. Nothing on this continent has ever come close to the meticulous cruelty of Apartheid. And yet, the country of Mandela has triumphed over it by walking the path of reconciliation. If, on the other hand, the Blacks from Soweto or Natal had decided to hunt down the Whites, nobody in the West would have condoned it. Nobody would have said: we must understand the wrath of the Blacks from Cape Town or Durban; it's a backlash against centuries of atrocities and humiliation, no matter whether they were imagined or real. And it is clear that the international community would have intervened immediately on behalf of those victims…

For all of us, the time spent in Rwanda has become an integral part of our lives, notwithstanding the fact that for each one of us, the experience was different. Some of us reacted with caution, while others used every opportunity to shout out in anger.[12]

The implication of the French government in the genocide has made me personally much more wary of the danger of being a small country under domination, as is the case with Senegal, where I come from. That also means I became more interested in the criminal tendencies of *Françafrique*.

We could not hope to get out of a country unscathed which was really just a huge cemetery and had chosen to leave some remains of the victims of the genocide exposed for everyone to see. It was so radically different from encountering reality through a book. We had to learn to listen to human beings who were irreparably broken, reciting our own novels to us before a single sentence had even been written down.

It was strange how we were wrestling with these figures of flesh and blood – our future characters – who were barely more credible than their stories.... It was not surprising that they saw us as potential traitors. Would we be able to tell their gruesome stories and speak for their dead, who were scattered everywhere and no-where?

Our only merit is that we have tried to do our best, despite the ambiguities of this undertaking. We have, I think, succeeded in giving a voice to the suffering of the Rwandan people insofar as this suffering directly concerns every human being on this planet. This claim to universality has given us the power to engrave the genocide into the Book of Time. Waiting to be read and commented on by students at schools and universities, our novels are at the start of a long journey through space and time. Other creative minds will draw inspiration from them, be it for a film or theatre adaptation, or for choreographic work.

Jean-Marie Vianney Rurangwa and Venuste Kayimahe, the two Rwandan authors in our group, contented themselves with writing down their thoughts, rather than creating fiction. I personally think that the great literary works about the genocide of April 1994 will be written later and that Rwandans will write them. Before this can happen, it is no doubt necessary for the process of grieving to be completed, for the pain to be distilled through several generations and for their sons and daughters, as they come out of a long stupor, to find the words at last which can tell the madness of their forefathers.

Yolande Mukagasana

Talking to the Killers…[13]

Rwanda 94, the play by Jacques Delcuvellerie starts with a young woman sitting in the twilight. She sounds surprisingly calm as she is describing what happened to her during April 1994. She says her name is Yolande Mukagasana and she is not acting. She is simply talking to a petrified audience about the lingering deaths of her husband Joseph Murekezi and their three children. She tells how her little Nadine, aged 13, was thrown alive into a communal ditch. She tells how Sandrine and Christian were savagely butchered with a machete. Which is the mass grave where their remains were scattered, amid screams of hate, among tens of thousands of dead bodies? She doesn't know, of course. Her testimony, candid, precise and detailed, could hardly be more moving.

Yolande Mukagasana rose to fame after the publication in 1997 of *Death Does Not Want Me*[14]. Like Venuste Kayimahe, Ntaribi Kamanzi and Benjamin Sehene, she is one of a number of Rwandans who refuse to just write off the one million genocide victims. Having escaped death by a hair's breadth, Yolande Mukagasana threw herself back into life several times over, with only one goal in mind: to bring the truth, and the whole truth, about the Hundred Days of Horror in Rwanda to the surface.

This battle has not only led her to the theatre; she has also taken an exhibition all over the world and roughly every other year, she has published a new book. The second one, *Don't Be Afraid to Know,*[15] is a remarkable call to transparency and courage. Wherever there is a debate going on about the subject, she is probably there, with facts and figures at her fingertips and exasperation in her voice, explaining how a modern State systematically prepared and then carried out the extermination of an entire section of its population. She is one of the survivors who simply won't buy the cliché that great pain is mute. People think she is mad when she stops strangers in the street and says to them, over and over again: "I, Yolande Mukagasana, have lost those dearest to me under the most horrendous circumstances during the genocide. I realize you don't know enough about it, but, no matter what you think, this concerns you, too." One has to admit that this is an unusual thing to do. On the other hand, at a time when so many do-gooders pretend to be distressed about human rights, it should perhaps have seemed quite natural. But one also has to bear in mind that these very rights are not the same for everybody. Listening to Yolande Mukagasana's sorrows only rarely succeeds in rousing a few people from their peaceful slumber.

Her crusade against oblivion may have earned her a few hate attacks, but more often, she has had to put up with glances that were either just mildly condescending or frankly appalled. Clearly, Yolande Mukagasana's fight seems completely pointless to many. This mother has lost her children? What a tragedy! It's amazing that she makes such a fuss about it in Africa, this place where thousands of people die every day for all sorts of weird and wonderful reasons.

The fact is that there are still many for whom the assassination of more than one million Rwandans does not represent such a big problem. Do they deserve to be called denialists? Not really: they are not denying anything. They are just busy doing more important things, that is all. It would simply have been too much trouble for them to protest against these undeniable, scandalous crimes.

The American Philip Gourevitch is not the only one to be taken aback by the total lack of ambiguity in the Rwandan Genocide.[16] Acting in broad daylight and supported by a radio channel and all the civilian and military resources of the State, the *genocidaires* never even tried to make a secret of their intentions. The knowledge that they could count on an ally as powerful as François Mitterrand, combined with the passivity of the international community, made them so cocksure of their success that it never occurred to them to cover their tracks. That is the reason why no serious intellectual has ever dared to question the enormity of the horror of these massacres. And yet, there is a kind of denial with respect to the Rwandan Genocide, which is purely *a matter of principle.* It is based on openly racist prejudices and has nothing to do with the objective reality of these recent events – a typical scenario when 'only Africa' is at stake. Nobody puts it better than Charles Pasqua who, at the end of June 1994, at the height of the killings, said on the

Eight o'clock News: "You know, it is important to understand that for those people, the abject horror of what happened has a totally different significance than for us."[17]

However, the perception that every Rwandan has been a killer at some point or another, forged into terse soundbites by a handful of intellectuals and popular politicians, is no less prevalent among Africans than in the rest of the world. This is based on the foregone conclusion that there is no need to even make the attempt to draw a dividing line between the guilty and the innocent. Since Africa is so widely seen as a continent in the grip of epidemics, tribal warfare and famine, we deny the genocide by suggesting that this was not really such an unusual occurrence and that it could just have happened by accident. And to portray Africa as a bloody shambles basically proves the point: it's too bad, but the place never changes.

So this is definitely no exaggeration: instead of saying that the genocide never happened, popular opinion claims that it happened twice and that each person caught up in it played both the roles of executioner and victim, one after the other. The Rwandan Genocide is without doubt the only one about which people are in denial by splitting it in two. When asked about it after the Franco-African summit in Biarritz, François Mitterrand returned the journalist's question sharply by saying: "The genocide or the genocides? I no longer know what to say!" He knew only too well. In his position and considering the close ties between the French government and the organizers of the genocide, he must have been one of the four or five personalities on the planet with first-hand information on the situation in Rwanda. It is certainly amazing to think that President Mitterrand's sincerity was just a sham and that he was playing word-games in a situation of such gravity. Similarly, a former UN Secretary General – who admittedly apologized later on – went there and said, with a little disillusioned sigh: "In Rwanda, the Hutus kill the Tutsis and the Tutsis kill the Hutus." But that is not all. In an outrageously bad book, spiked with blatant inaccuracies, a certain former French minister – of co-operation, no less – proudly announces his intention to tell, at last, "the true story of the Rwandan Genocides."[18] Underlying all these pronouncements is a negrophobia so well concealed that it is not even aware of itself anymore. One can explain this by saying that intentionally or not, in a poor African country under foreign rule very little value is attached to human life.

This thought pattern dictates that those who died in Rwanda simply didn't have the time to strike first in the course of these eternal "interethnic massacres" which have become so tiresome for the rest of the world. Visitors making a daytrip to Nyamata have been overheard asking whether the bodies which are exposed in the church have perhaps been transported there by the new authorities in Kigali, after the genocide, in order to mystify foreigners like themselves... Under different circumstances, obscene remarks of this kind would definitely have discredited those who made them.

The economy in the broader sense of the term is frequently evoked – with particular reference to demographic pressures – as a possible explanation for the extent of the massacres. This is not acceptable: nowhere can poverty be used as an excuse when human beings degenerate into raging, senseless hyenas. Every individual who considers himself human is duty-bound to do his utmost to comprehend fully the sequence of events which brought about this tragedy. But such an endeavour must start with the precept that what happened in Rwanda in 1994 constituted an ignominious transgression. Refusing to admit this is virtually like saying that *in certain parts of the world, there is no difference between life and death.* Every African must ask himself why perfectly normal fathers and mothers and their families all over the world burst into tears when something happens to their pets, but seem so cold and detached when confronted with the dead bodies of children from Rwanda.

One can immediately see how profoundly different Yolande Mukagasana and Venuste Kayimahe are from certain commentators who are just a little bit too *cool.* Those dead bodies the racists spit upon with so much disdain are, quite simply, their own flesh and blood.

Of course, one ought not to generalize. Right here in Africa, intellectuals, maybe because they are not well informed or because they are increasingly succumbing to self-denigration, have reacted to this genocide either with stubborn silence or with indifference. Even taking Nelson Mandela's indignation and the reports written by professor René Degni-Ségui or by the OAU into account, the impact of the Rwandan tragedy on this continent is in no way commensurate to its immeasurable excesses. *Rwanda, a French Genocide,*[19] by Mehdi Bah, remains, to our knowledge, an exception in francophone Africa.

Outside Rwanda itself, reflection about the issue has mainly taken place in Europe and in America, thanks to the books by Jean-Pierre Chrétien,[20] Gérard Prunier,[21] François-Xavier Verschave,[22] Patrick de Saint-Exupéry[23] and Colette Braeckmann.[24] The fact that the Belgian photographer Alain Kazinierakis co-authored Yolande Mukagasana's third book clearly shows that the universal character of the genocide is not lost on the rest of the world. In numerous other publications, intellectuals of all colours, journalists, academics and human rights organizations let the survivors speak. The stories of these survivors are at the same time austere and unbearable. The individual genocide accounts all follow more or less the same narrative outline: on the evening of April 6, 1994, president Habyarimana's aeroplane was shot down and thirty minutes later, the first barricades started going up. The moderate Hutu leaders were liquidated with the help of lists that had been drawn up in advance, and then the killing of all the Tutsis, regardless of sex, age or political opinion, began.

Death, Despair, Defiance,[25] published in London from May 1994 onwards by African Rights and *No Witness Must Survive*[26] are typical of this genre. Here, survivors speak about how they have had to watch their loved-ones die. While they are talking, one feels immediately how they are still reeling from the shock of their violent emotions, the majority of these testimonies having been recorded just a few weeks or even only a few days after the last massacres.

It is easy to imagine the sense of outrage and disbelief of those who had to collect these field reports. Their status as foreigners made it especially hard for them to eschew the distortions, misunderstandings, or even manipulations that can be inherent in the seemingly straightforward transfer of one language into another.

And one can understand why some of the survivors wanted to spare themselves the pain of having their wounds opened up all over again. Still deeply traumatized by their sufferings, they are simply longing to forget their recent past and to turn to the future, for better or for worse.

The work of the Rwandan intellectuals can probably be best described as an important effort at rationalization. José Kagabo, Benjamin Sehene,[27] Jean-Marie Vianney Rurangwa,[28] Josias Semunjanga and many others have revisited the genocide, each one of them analyzing what happened on the basis of their personal experiences and in that way, helping us in our task of mapping its contours in detail. Considering the extent of the tragedy, though, direct eyewitness accounts, collected by Rwandans for the information of the world at large, have remained very few.[29]

Yolande Mukagasana's book is one of the first attempts to fill this gap. A photograph of the survivor or prisoner who has told his or her story accompanies each testimony. The pictures by Alain Kazineriakis, who, with Yolande Mukagasana, went to the hills and to the prisons of Rwanda, give this book a special dimension. Its gripping images show the wounds of people we don't know, who speak to us and who in this way have had their humanity restored to them. But, looking at them also brings out the voyeur in us, whether we like it or not. The reader is so dumbfounded that in order to soothe the distress these flashbacks are causing him, he will want to study the expression on each one of these faces in detail. He will probably spend longer looking at the assassins, so great is his desire – or his hope – to discover even a trace of humanity in the eyes of the *genocidaire.*

And even if there are many accounts by survivors in *The Wounds of Silence,* one understands very quickly that what makes this book so unusual is what the killers have to say. The elaborate excuses of the executioners overlap, in a fascinating long-distance dialogue, with the memories of their victims.

And one of the latter is Yolande Mukagasana herself…

She has gone to the local prison to meet some of the *genocidaires,* most of whom have decided to plead guilty. The fact that she is a survivor herself changes her relationship with them completely.

The language she uses when she speaks to them is very simple, with words which they have no choice but to understand instantly: "You have to admit that you are a part of the problem and that, if you don't explain why you have committed these acts, nobody will ever understand what has happened." That is her way of reminding them of their duty to humanity, to which they themselves still belong, despite the crimes they have committed.

She and the murderers know each other very well. They are on first-name terms and sometimes Yolande Mukagasana shouts at them. Slowly but surely it becomes clear that this is the next episode of her own story. Nothing points to it unequivocally, but it is possible and even likely that the monsters she has chosen to confront include those who lifted their hand against her husband Joseph or her children. Everybody should make up his or her own mind about this, after reading her conversation with a certain Enos N.

"Do you know Ngenzi Déo?" Yolande Mukagasana asks him.

"The sculptor? Yes, I know him very well", answers the other one.

Then Yolande Mukagasana tells him quietly: "He was my father." The other one, crying out in terror:

"Your father? Does that mean Musoni is your brother?"

"Yes", says Yolande.

After a brief silence, the assassin panics and declares with comical gravity: "I solemnly swear, Madam, I never killed anybody in your family."

Besides the totally misplaced humour in this exchange, it gives an idea of what a country is like where the question of who has killed whom continues to weigh so heavily on even the simplest human relationships. It has often been said that the paths of executioner and victim are continuing to cross in silence on the hills of Rwanda. Up to now, one used to think of them casting sombre glances at each other before continuing on their way. But this very unusual book is so far unique in making the encounter take place right in front of us, and, instead of shying away from the reality of the genocide, here, Rwandans choose to talk about it without hatred, but with a frankness which sometimes borders on being brutal.

The dialogue Yolande Mukagasana has chosen to attribute to the *genocidaires* is true and profoundly meaningful for the whole of humanity. And in a certain way, it also helps articulate the revenge of the weak. During the genocide, the killers would arrive on their doorstep, drowning them in profanities and completely deaf to their futile pleadings to let them live. How, in fact, can we really talk to each other while "the machetes are singing", to put it in the words of Chadian playwright Koulsy Lamko. In *The Wounds of Silence,* the relationship has been totally reversed. Here it is the perpetrators who are protesting their innocence. Some of them are getting caught up in preposterous lies and feeble denials, but on the whole, their remorse reflects a moving sincerity.

Yolande Mukagasana is so powerful, because there is not even one moment when she plays the game of scientific neutrality. And how could she, anyway? Rwanda is her country and every testimony brings back her own personal pain. She knows what it means to be hiding somewhere, listening to the sounds of death prowling all around her. She is not just a journalist from a far-away country who is easily misled. For Yolande Mukagasana, just listening is not enough, and she hasn't come to take notes which she is going to brush up later. In other words, she wants to speak aloud the uncomfortable truth, not write perfectly honed sentences.

And since she knows as much about their heinous crimes as the killers themselves, she never hesitates to astound them. When Gaspard B is suffering from a sudden bout of amnesia, she reminds him, mercilessly, "It was you who forced my children out of their hiding place." And she ends another such conversation by furiously spitting at someone by the name of Marc, "I am not listening to your lies for another minute. You have told me nothing but lies, from beginning to end and this is intolerable for me."

The proximity of Yolande Mukagasana to all the people with whom she is conducting these conversations, makes her book a great beacon of truth about the Rwandan Genocide. They entrust themselves to her completely and things are spelled out in this book which have never been said anywhere else. One must not forget that Yolande Mukagasana is a midwife by profession. And as a matter of fact, that was her profession in another life, *in her previous life.* She can wait patiently for a confession to come when the time is right, since she has not forgotten the art of midwifery. So it happens that, during their second encounter, a *genocidaire* by the name of Sylvester says to her sheepishly: "I lied to you the other day." With this confession, a psychological obstacle is removed and their relationship improves. Her partners in these exchanges, both the survivors and the perpetrators, come from all layers of Rwandan society. In this book, prisoners as notorious as Valéry Bameriki, from the sinister RTLM, rub shoulders with Rwandans of all ages and all walks of life. Those at the bottom of the social ladder of course tend to be most inclined to regret their crimes and ask their victims for forgiveness. Among them is a ten-year-old kid who has killed other children and who knows that his mother went insane; or there is Ancilla, who "out of love" made her four Tutsi children drink insecticide and who says to Yolande: "They are all dead and today I envy them." Faustin M. pleads guilty as well, but doesn't seem very tortured by his remorse: "I killed ten people, four of whom paid me five thousand Francs each for the permission to commit suicide. The money, I can't really remember what I used it for." Sylvester – yes it's him again – has written some poems while he was in prison, which say that "even the good have become bad," while in another one he rambles on about the afterlife, holding the skull of one of his victims in his hand. And there is one assassin who nearly lost his mind. Yolande admits that she gave him milk and two bananas…

Contrary to what one might think, Yolande Mukagasana did not go and taunt the *genocidaires* in their prison cells. What she did was guided by her need to mend the broken strands of her own life, rather like a strange love towards these victims of another species, the deplorable survivors of the trap of hate. This results in a number of slightly hackneyed dialogues about the future of mankind, about religion and about life. ("At any rate, I am dead, too," Évariste confides to her. He is a young prisoner who was forced by adults to kill his playmates). The tone becomes almost biblical when Yolande Mukagasana tries to comfort one of the *genocidaires* who is remorseful and on the verge of despair. She is clearly shaken as she says to him: "And I, Mathieu, I am telling you that you are alive because now you know where the evil is, you are asking for forgiveness and you want to work for peace between the people of Rwanda."

As for the survivors' testimonies, they are all absolutely unbearable. Even for those who think they know all about the killers and their sordid creativity, *The Wounds of Silence* will not make easy reading. The voices one hears in this book, forceful and vulnerable at the same time, are not paper voices. One of them belongs to Victoire who was raped by a horde of men she did not know. "They smelt of dirt, the forest and blood," she says. Her baby, tied to a tree, was devoured alive by a dog, with her torturer looking on, visibly amused. Then there is Clémence, who was also raped for days on end, "in a house infested with rats and fleas." Yolande Mukagasana, suddenly furious with rage, calls Diane, the little girl who was born as a result of this, "the product of humiliation, a cross between hatred and suffering." Eugénie N., thirty-two years old, erupts, letting off a salvo which seems to have risen from the depths of a grave: "I was covered in maggots, I even ate some of them, because they were in my mouth." The long and impressive account by Brother Damascène – doctor of psychology and survivor of all the massacres since 1959 – shows very clearly that the genocide of 1994 was not the sudden awakening of an atavistic bloodlust, but the result of several decades of systematic preparation. A simple testimony can say so much more about this than all the learned volumes that deal with the logic of radical extermination and genocide. A young woman by the name of Francine M. describes how mayor Jean-Paul Akayesu was distributing machetes and saying that "the children who are going to be born should have to ask their parents what a Tutsi looked like and that every Tutsi woman should be undressed so that one can see what her genitals and her thighs are like since they will soon be wiped off the face of the earth." A few sentences are enough to prove that, despite all its flimsy denials, the French government was in the same camp as mayor Akayesu who presided over collective rapes followed by killing sprees during which he jokingly reprimanded his subjects, his pinkie in the air, "My children, you must never come and ask me again what the genitals of a Tutsi woman look like."

The former mayor of Giti, the only place in Rwanda that managed to escape the massacres, explains this old Franco-Rwandan "Brotherhood in Arms." "France", he says during his conversation with Yolande Mukagasana, "became involved in the war in Rwanda before the genocide. It was French soldiers who verified the identity cards and they were on the battle fields." Dozens of other testimonies, some of them from very young children, talk at length about what *Operation Turquoise* was really like. All this is true and will surely be re-told one day.

Following other authors, Jean-Paul Gouteux has widened the gap by publishing *The Dark Night of Rwanda*,[30] which perhaps some follower of General Aussaresses is going to fill one day.

Yolande Mukagasana, meanwhile, is attacking the monster through another one of her voices. By letting the victims and the repentant perpetrators speak, all of whom have been profoundly crippled by what they have been through, she is above all seeking to heal her compatriots' trauma. There is a passage in *The Wounds of Silence*, which says that the *genocidaires* did not expect to ever have to justify their acts, for the simple reason that not a single Tutsi would be left among the living to accuse them. This book puts a final stamp on the failure of this insane plan.

The Wounds of Silence is not only an exceptional historical document. It also has a lot to do with the *gacaca*,[31] those inevitably painful talks that are meant to help a bruised country free itself of the historical traps laid by the self-serving conqueror.

Kigali–Paris

The Two-Headed Monster

"Oh yes…! The Tutsis of Rwanda! The people who use the genocide to justify their own cruelty, right?" It is 1998, we are in a small town in the canton Aargau and the person talking, with the ice tinkling softly in his whisky glass, is a young man from Zurich, director of an NGO for development aid. Eight years after this little interlude, I have still neither understood nor forgotten the hostile expression in Benedict's impenetrable grey eyes that so startled me at the time. How was it possible for something that had happened four years earlier in a place as far away as Rwanda, to be so unnerving for a Swiss citizen who otherwise seemed to have no particular problems? Just a few minutes earlier, I had been listening to Benedict boasting about his travels across Africa. He was one of those strange people who are constantly trying to convince you that the situation on our continent is robbing them of their sleep, while suggesting at the same time that you yourself are perfectly resigned to the cruel fate of your brothers. The man certainly hadn't been lazy: he had set up a well at Abéché, two health stations in Diourbel, a conflict prevention centre in Maputo and more… He had also criss-crossed Rwanda when, nicknamed the Switzerland of Africa, it was still the playground of Western NGOs. For all these reasons, I should have found the man I was talking to terrific. He obviously thought that all these charitable acts entitled him to the blatant honesty that one may, at a pinch, find among close friends. So he insisted on making his irritation with 'that whole genocide story' (sic) very clear. And too bad for you if you didn't agree with him. There was something rather disturbing about the fact that he did not seem too bothered by the mass graves of Kibungo while he was leading his cosy little life in the comfort and prosperity of Helvetia.

And Benedict's name was really just the first on a long list of denialists that I have encountered over the last few years.

I remember a post-conference dinner on the campus of Louvain-la-Neuve. With a devilish grin, the professor who had invited me to his class simply couldn't stop joking, in his nasal voice, about the 'veneer of Christianity' of the Rwandan people. To him, there was something almost funny about this rather garish genocide where the not-so-catholic church members hadn't found it much of a problem to bump off their brothers in faith. Being reminded of the attitude of the Vatican during the Holocaust was clearly a lot less amusing for him. We ended up hurling insults at each other and he was so furious that he pointedly handed back the copy of *Murambi: The Book of Bones,* to the lady-friend who had just given it to him. A very strange fellow he was, this Prof. When during his class, I said Mudimbé was one of my favourite authors, he literally choked: "But he moved to the US, that guy, and makes a point of writing exclusively in English now!" I understood then that the 'betrayal' of this Zaïrean novelist was all the more odious to him since he was an alumnus of Louvain-la-Neuve...

Franco-African literature is strewn with these lovesick warriors of the lecture theatres and their total infatuation with the language of Molière....

Do I have to mention again the French editor who couldn't bear the fact that in the preface to one of Yolande Mukagasana's books I had placed the name of François Mitterrand next to those of some notorious *genocidaires*? Despite Yolande's protestations, he said brusquely: "It will either be the book without the preface or no book at all". And he stuck to it.

This kind of incident is by no means unusual, by the way. If an African shows an interest in the Rwandan Genocide, he will find that he is constantly being handed a mirror, with an invitation to face his demons.

When in 1994 Yvonne Mutimura-Galinier, whose entire family had just been assassinated, sought refuge at the Hotel Mille Collines, a French official said to her scornfully: "The hotel will be attacked, and everybody will be killed; that's your barbarism, that's your history, now fight your war".[32]

A few weeks after the genocide, François Mitterrand expressed the same idea in terms that were nearly as harsh: "What can France possibly do if African chiefs decide to solve their problems with the machete?"[33]

That is really the position of the *Quilès Commission*[34]: 'Rwanda responsible for its own history'.

All these statements imply that: 'They have been killing each other again, these Africans, and, as usual, they want us to take the blame. We're not going to let them get away with that'. The trap in this argument is so cunningly laid that it rules out an analysis of the political mechanisms which so evidently were the root cause of the Rwandan blood bath right from the start.

The ringleaders, very far away from the arena where the action was and their local accomplices, can sleep easy. Any attempt to throw light on the role of certain Western powers in this tragedy will be interpreted as a ('typically African') refusal to take responsibility.

The logic behind this is simply not watertight. Since it is difficult to refute the historical facts that incriminate certain Western countries, one hides behind a vague moral principle ('It's no good trying to pass the buck') to dodge potentially embarrassing questions. In the following pages, we will be careful to avoid the pitfall of abstract speculation (about 'guilt', 'innocence', 'colonial heritage' etc.). We will remind ourselves of specific events which are verifiable and have exact dates. But just to establish these facts is obviously not enough. The background to all this is of course the political doctrine denying Africans the right to independence and to dispose of their resources as they see fit.

It is not easy to maintain today that the history of the Rwandan Genocide is not well known. Thousands of books have been written on it by academics, journalists and eyewitnesses, both Rwandan and non-Rwandan. Filmmakers and playwrights are especially interested in it, which allows the wider public to form their own, more or less accurate opinion about the topic. And above and beyond that, a number of concerned Western countries, important Human Rights organizations and the international community have conducted inquiries into it.[35]

All these reports have been available from libraries and online for several years, and even if they haven't answered every single question, they are nevertheless precious tools for all those who are keen to acquire an objective opinion about the events in Rwanda. One of these reports was compiled on the initiative of the Organization of African Unity (OAU), and bears the evocative title *Rwanda: The Avoidable Genocide.*[36]

While the results of this report were presented to the press on July 10, 2000, Stephen Lewis, one of the members of the organization, was particularly harsh towards Madeleine Albright, the American representative at the UN at the time: "The role of the United States in this Rwandan affair [...] has been an unbelievable disgrace. I don't know how Madeleine Albright manages to live with this on her conscience", were his exact words. The Canadian diplomat thus underlined the fact that Ms. Albright had done everything in her power to prevent an intervention by the UN in Rwanda, right to the end.

It was vital for the US to avoid the use of the term 'genocide', which due to the Geneva Convention of 1948 would have necessitated military action.

The reason for such extreme caution was that one year earlier on October 3, 1993, the mutilated bodies of nineteen marines had been dragged through the streets of Mogadishu by a furious crowd of Somalians.

This caused an immense shock and meant that America lost all desire to send its *boys* to Africa. One can sum up the situation like this: in order to protect the lives of a few professional soldiers, the Clinton administration had no compunction to let hundreds of thousands of Rwandans perish.[37]

Was it actually possible to be more cynical than that? It was indeed and the country giving concrete proof of this is President Mitterrand's France. There is no book on this topic, however biased, that doesn't demonstrate in the most staggering way sometimes that France was actively and resolutely implicated in the Rwandan Genocide. The OAU report is a case in point. Nobody could possibly claim that the Eminent Persons' Group, which compiled it, was in some way prejudiced against France. Apart from perhaps one or two exceptions, its members have the sort of background that ensures they are completely unbiased towards France and its Africa policy.

This notwithstanding, the conclusions of this very well argued and seriously documented report are an indictment for Paris.[38]

Never having been a French colony, Rwanda made its entry into the "pré-carré" in July 1973, after Juvénal Habyarimana's coup d'état. Since then, France has maintained very strong economic and military ties with this tiny, allegedly francophone neighbour of the enormously large and prosperous Zaïre.

Apart from some less important operations, Noroît, Amaryllis and Turquoise were started there and this is where the country's killer militias as well as its regular army were trained.

The question of whether the Interahamwe[39] militiamen received special French military training continues to be hotly debated. One has to understand that in this particular case, the honour of the French army is at stake... Unfortunately for it, tongues have started wagging in the army's inner circles. And so it was that chief warrant officer Thierry Prugnaud of the GIGN made some interesting revelations to the journalist Laure de Vulpian on France Culture. It was on Friday, April 22, 2005. His statements are irrefutable: he was in Rwanda in 1992, and he saw his colleagues instructing the killers in the Akagera National Park: "I say this publicly and categorically because I saw them...They had to be militiamen because the military are all in combat uniform over there. I attest that the French military trained Rwandan militiamen. I think this dragged on until 1994", says the non-commissioned officer without beating about the bush, and perfectly spontaneously, he adds that when it comes to the genocide in Rwanda, the French army 'denies a lot of things.'

And this is really the crux of the matter: they also 'deny' having continued to channel supplies to the Rwandan army in a clandestine manner at the very time when the genocide was being perpetrated. The OAU report catches them in the act of lying repeatedly and mentions the revelations of the commander of the Belgian contingent of the Minuar, which were widely exposed in the international press at the time. Colonel Luc Marchal claims to have witnessed how, under the pretence of evacuating French nationals, the military was delivering ammunition to the government clique of *genocidaires.* He happened to be at Kigali airport at the beginning of the genocide, watching the arrival of the three first French aeroplanes: "Two of these three planes," he would say later, "were transporting personnel. And the third one was carrying ammunition [...] for the Rwandan army [...]. They stayed at the aerodrome for a few minutes and then immediately [the ammunition] was loaded onto vehicles which were driven to the camp [of Kanombé]." [40]

The report is just as detailed when it comes to the impact of the French forces on the whole process leading up to the genocide. One reads there that "the French troops had been present since 1990, when until the arrival of the first contingents of the Minuar in December 1993, they were playing a central role in preventing a quick victory by the RPF.[41] It was at that point that the French soldiers left the country, leaving an undercover intelligence team behind."

It would have been difficult for them to make their loyalties clearer than that. But in the end, none of this prevented the defeat of the protégés of Paris, who were so preoccupied with slitting children's throats that they didn't get round to taking on the RPF. When the French government, which had until then opposed any intervention by the international community, realized they were losing, they suddenly announced their intention, in June 1994, to send troops to Rwanda for 'humanitarian reasons'.

As many commentators pointed out with bitter irony at the time, there was barely anyone left to save. Those familiar with the Rwanda file knew, without a shadow of doubt, that France had a secret agenda, and a total detachment from any respect for human life whatsoever. The OAU report brings to mind the view of a scholar who writes that "for centuries, throughout the entire duration of the Slave Trade and the colonial era, 'every imperialist intervention [in Africa] was staged under the pretence of humanitarian intervention.'"

And according to the historian Gérard Prunier,[42] this sudden change of attitude was actually due to Nelson Mandela, the first democratically elected president of South Africa, who had announced his intention to send troops to Rwanda in order to put an end to the killings. This news must have spread panic among the strategists in Paris – under no circumstances could the Anglo-Saxon enemy be allowed to intrude into the francophone backyard.

In next to no time, 2,300 men were ready to be dispatched to Rwanda. They were heavily armed, because, unusually, the Security Council had authorized Turquoise to intervene under the articles of chapter 7. This means they could open fire if it was deemed necessary, something the actual UN forces, the Minuar, under the command of the Canadian General Romeo Dallaire, were not allowed to do! The latter, beside himself with fury, threatened to shoot down the French planes, should they come "to deliver their infernal weapons to the government". A government intent on genocide, of course.

Dallaire's statement is added proof that nobody really trusted France in this affair. It also seems that Turquoise constituted a compromise between the faction in the French coalition government intent on a military assault on Kigali and the Prime Minister, Édouard Balladur, who was far more reserved. The final result was predictable: according to the OAU report, 'the analysts indicated that the French intervention might have saved between 10,000 and 15,000 Tutsis, and not "tens of thousands," as President Mitterrand had proclaimed; a commendable achievement, certainly, while his other task was to sustain the interim government.

Some authorities actually believe that the humanitarian aspect of this mission was merely a smoke screen created by France in order to preserve an area of the country for the plans of the regime of the *genocidaires* and its collaborators, "killers included," who were invading the region in large numbers ahead of the advancing RPF.

When it became clear that it would be impossible to halt the advance of the RPF, France kept its cool and facilitated the escape of the majority of the Hutu extremist ringleaders to Zaïre. Africa is still paying for this today and the *genocidaires* were able to continue the fight. The fact that so many Hutu extremists managed to flee to Zaïre, aided and abetted by France, was undoubtedly the most significant occurrence in the entire Great Lakes region after the genocide and set in motion a chain of events which would eventually engulf the whole area in the conflict.' This passage deserves consideration by every advocate of the theory of the "double genocide"...

Operation Turquoise has also been implicated in: the transportation of governmental military detachments towards the Zaïrean border in French army vehicles; the delivery of ten million tons of food supplies to Goma, destined for the ex-FAR troops and – in the same town – delivery of "five consignments of weapons [which were] expedited from France to Goma during May and June, while the genocide was in full swing."[43]

Instead of fading away, the initial suspicions about Operation Turquoise have only deepened over the years. Some of its members have been accused of having behaved like brothers in arms of the Interahamwe and of having divulged the Tutsi hiding places to them. Furthermore, there is increasing evidence of the active participation of French soldiers in the fighting during the genocide, especially in Bisesero, one of the few places in Rwanda where the Tutsis were trying to organize their resistance... Precisely this is implied in a dispatch from Associated Press on March 26, 2004, which also mentions the "Citizens' Commission of Inquiry". In addition, charges have been laid against the members of Turquoise by a group of survivors. Even if there is perhaps little chance of this legal action being successful, there is hope that in the course of the proceedings at least some of the historical truth will be re-established.

The culmination of this abominable moral failure was – not really surprisingly – Mitterrand pictured side by side with Mobutu during the Franco-African summit at Biarritz in November 1994.

He knew that having questions thrown at him was going to be inevitable and when asked, he replied with perfect nonchalance: "Which genocide would you like to talk about, Sir...? The one by the Hutus against the Tutsis, or the one by the Tutsis against the Hutus?"

And apparently, a few minutes later, thinking he was out of earshot of the reporters, he turned to a member of his entourage with the words: "That journalist who was trying to interrogate me about Rwanda, I certainly shut him up, didn't I?"

All this is simply below the belt and it is difficult to believe that the issue here is the death of more than one million innocent people.

The speaker here is the only head of state on the planet the *genocidaires* did not dare disobey. With one phone call, President Mitterrand could have saved hundreds of thousands of human lives. He didn't do it.

"In those countries down there, a genocide isn't that important". Hindsight makes it easier to see what sort of consequences this sentence, attributed to Mitterrand, has had. His way of talking cast him in the role of the high-powered action-man who deals harshly with the softies in his camp reassuring them that whatever happens, he has the situation under control. The words have not been pronounced, but one can almost hear them, somehow echoing the voice of Mitterrand: this is our Africa; we know what to do. And as if that were not enough, he also prided himself on having a sense of history. Of course it's true that his country has always managed pretty well: apart from the lost wars in Algeria and Indochina, France can only congratulate itself on the positive aspects of its... decolonization. South of the Sahara, with few exceptions, the political élite has always been at its beck and call, without being shown any sign of gratitude, as one can read and hear in the negrophobic discourse since the genocide. In *The Dark Night of Rwanda*,[44] the late Jean-Paul Gouteux recalls a number of statements by Bruno Delaye, François Mitterrand's African Affairs advisor during the genocide.

When he is questioned by Alison des Forges on behalf of Human Rights Watch at a later stage, he deplores the massacres and enlightens us on the sociological angle of the issue, which one can sum up as follows: "Africans are like that". And when in January 1998, the journalist Patrick de Saint-Exupéry was retrospectively amazed that he received ministers of the Kigali regime while the hills of Rwanda were littered with hundreds of thousands of bodies, he said, cynically: "Since my arrival, I must have dealt with four hundred assassins and two thousand drug dealers. In Africa, it's impossible not to get one's hands dirty."[45]

It is also interesting to note that on the topic of Rwanda, even the revisionist never denies anything. On the contrary, he has the extremely odd feeling that, the more gruesome details he adds to the catalogue of horrors, the more innocent he is himself. Yes of course, in this African country, ten thousand people were killed every day for three months. So what? That's what happens in Africa. France can't be held responsible for such a calamity. In 2003, Dominique de Villepin,[46] who was minister of Foreign Affairs at the time, expressed his distress "about the terrible genocides which Rwanda has had to endure" in a similar vein. And how many genocides are we talking about, M. de Villepin? Two. It's a well known fact that when it comes to bloodshed, Africans never do things by halves. The theory of the double genocide has many advantages. It allows the kind-hearted humanitarian to show sympathy to *all* the victims, while at the same time sidelining the specific case of Rwanda in such a way that a strict, universally valid moral code no longer applies.

It is not the first time that the French have sided with the wrong camp in Africa, but they have generally managed to get away with rather feeble excuses and by counting on the inertia of their accusers.

In Rwanda itself on the other hand, France has unfortunately been associated with the ultimate criminal act. And every time the subject is mentioned, Paris is directly implicated – even their Western allies are sniggering behind their back. This time, it's impossible to get out of it by just letting the storm pass. What attempts have been made to regain control have found expression in a number of books in the spirit of a revisionism which can only be described as candid and somewhat desperate, but above all as an insult for the victims. Almost all their authors are interested in the bomb attack of April 6, 1994. They claim that Paul Kagame's Rwandan Patriotic Front (RPF) is solely to blame for the genocide and that he triggered it intentionally by shooting down President Juvénal Habyarimana's Falcon 50 on its way back from Arusha. This is an extremely serious allegation, but to this day we have no proof of the culpability of the RPF, despite the efforts – and the enormous resources… – of those whom it would suit very well.

On November 23, 2006, Judge Jean-Louis Bruguière charged Paul Kagame and nine of his closest associates with the attack that cost Juvénal Habyarimana his life. Since Kagame was under the protection of his presidential immunity, the United Nations had to be approached so that he could be referred to the International Criminal Tribunal for Rwanda in Arusha. International warrants of arrest were issued against the others. This judgment becomes a problem whenever a Commission of Inquiry is in Kigali in order to investigate the role of France in the genocide and gets to the point where it wants to press formal charges. It has also become known that in Paris itself, legal action was taken against other French citizens. Therefore, France had to respond.

What remains striking, however, is the lack of reaction from the international community to an issue as important as the indictment of a foreign president. Indeed, every time the French government takes action regarding the genocide it hits the same obstacle, and that is the poor credibility it enjoys in this matter. And besides, the news had barely hit the headlines when the daily *Le Monde* wrote: "Errors and doubtful testimonies affect the evidence of the French judiciary", indicating that "a large number of witnesses did not actually witness the facts and conversations they are reporting". And according to the French national evening paper "the inquiry puts forward the testimonies of senior ex-officers of the Rwandan armed forces. Yet what the text sometimes omits is that most of them have been convicted for their participation in the genocide by the Arusha International Criminal Tribunal for Rwanda. "That is the level of accuracy one is dealing with."[47]

A few days later, the journal *Libération* discovered that a witness by the name of Ruzigana, who was "frequently mentioned by Bruguière in his verdict, accused the magistrate of distorting his testimony in order to make it match his investigations." Here is the account the witness gave of his hearing. Having been contacted by *Libération* in Norway, Emmanuel Ruzigana, 35, gave a certain number of disturbing details. To start with, Ruzigana hardly spoke any French and even less English. And yet, according to the transcript of the hearing, dated March 29, 2004, 3:40p.m., a copy of which was made available to *Libération,* only three people were present: the judge, the clerk of the court Sandrine Mounes and the witness. No Kinyarwanda translator! Nevertheless, the answers given by the witness were in excellent French and very detailed. Today, Ruzigana explains that the clerk was reading a text and was asking him to say yes or no. "Sometimes I didn't understand the question and we had to go backwards and forwards several times. The judge didn't like my answers. At the end, he became irritated and said to me: "That's it, get out and you're not getting asylum!" Before she left, the clerk of the court very quickly read out the transcript and asked him to sign it. He obeyed, but didn't understand.

Afterwards, the daily reported under which circumstances this precious witness arrived in Paris two and a half years earlier. According to *Libération,* one of his compatriots called Ruzibiza "suggested that he should go to the French Embassy in Tanzania, where a certain 'Pierre' would give him a visa for France which indeed he obtained without difficulty. On his arrival in Paris, on March 29, 2004, he was met and taken to the judge under police escort."[48] It seems very unlikely that France had anything to do with the bomb attack of April 6, 1994. But it is all the more astonishing that France is trying to reduce the genocide to this incident only. The determination to incriminate the RPF without the slightest proof is not as absurd as it seems. In fact, it is a means of passing over in silence certain potentially very embarrassing questions for Paris. On the other hand, the following allegation deserves our attention for a moment: the idea that a liberation movement has voluntarily offered up one million people for slaughter in order to secure control over Rwanda, is profoundly racist. It is based on the idea that Africans – and their "chiefs", in the Mitterrandian sense of the term – are capable of the worst atrocities in order to gain, or hold on to, power. Those who ascribe such an agenda to the RPF don't really believe it themselves. But they know Africa has such a negative reputation that they will get away with it. The analogy with the Holocaust, which is often obvious in connection with the Rwandan Genocide, is undeniable here. There have been times when the Jews have been blamed for their own suffering. The journalist Olivier Guland became interested in what he calls the "affirmationism" of certain French "thinkers" of the extreme Right. Here is what he says: "Rather than denying or challenging reality, they consider the Final Solution and the figures in the history books as a fact, but they pretend that the Jews were massacred… at their own request in order to achieve their goal, world domination!"[49] Guland then gives a summary of the ramblings of a certain André Figueras: "As early as 1942, it became clear to the American Jews how much they could capitalize on the war in Europe. They therefore spurred on the Nazis in the radicalization of their anti-Semitic policies, pushing them to mass murder and trying to dissuade the Allies from bombarding the death camps in order not to interrupt the genocide".

And later, speaking about the discovery of these camps after the conflict, "the world, horrified by this tragedy and gripped by unspeakable remorse, abandoned anti-Judaism forever and bowing respectfully before the martyrdom of this people, went as far as offering them the very world domination they had been awaiting two thousand years." Anyone can see that this is utter lunacy and you would only find this sort of gibberish in an obscure fascist Parisian weekly. But when the Tutsis are discussed in terms that are nearly as insane, they are reported as if it were the most normal thing in the world, by supposedly reputable media channels earnestly pretending to weigh up all the pros and cons. Nothing is considered more legitimate than trying to throw light on the bomb attack of April 6, but one simply cannot reduce the genocide to this particular incident, however important it may be. To do this would be tantamount to the allegation – as Patrick de Saint-Exupéry has noted[50]– that the burning of the Reichstag was the cause of the Shoah and to using this as an excuse for the Nazi atrocities. Even the national interest cannot justify such an egregious insult on the memory of the dead.

This way of dealing with the aftermath of the genocide is akin to the logic which has prompted certain French decision makers to conclude at some point: "After all, this is only Africa, we can do there as we please; our compatriots don't care." It is true that the average Frenchman has difficulty distinguishing between the Democratic Republic of Congo and Congo-

Brazzaville, or between Chad and Benin, or even Eritrea. He hears the sounds of these exotic names ringing in his ears and for him they are so many dark countries, continually at war, since the dawn of time. And why? Nobody knows. These wars are completely pointless and the Africans, they are like children who simply have to fight. If you try to explain that things are not quite as simple as that, no one will listen to you. There are extremely refined and sophisticated people in France who are convinced that their government is not sending troops to Africa to defend their economic interests, but exclusively to prevent the Africans from killing each other. I have heard that a thousand times in connection with Ivory Coast, coming from sensible and genuinely sincere people. It is so absurd that it leaves you speechless.

It often happens that people take me aside and ask what interest France could possibly have had in Rwanda? This question, asked in an indignant tone, insinuates that this stronghold of human rights simply *could not* be guilty of complicity in the genocide. So the issue remains that we need to establish whether, *in reality*, France has been *rightly or wrongly* accused. It is preposterous to maintain that something which actually happened did not take place just because it doesn't agree with the idea, which is in fact erroneous, that one has of a country!

If one truly wants to know what motivated the responsible French authorities at the time, the simplest way – and that is also the civic duty of everybody on the electoral roll in the Hexagon – is to question them directly. As an outsider, it is perhaps just permissible to make a few observations. What is really at stake here is not so much Rwanda itself – a tiny country of no strategic interest – as the role played by France on the continent. At face-value, the case is simple: a client-state is attacked by a guerrilla force from an English-speaking country and all that matters is that the other French-speaking countries receive a clear message of absolute loyalty.

And we say: OK then, all this is well and good. But how is one expected to understand that this logic has been pushed all the way to complicity in genocide? That is the crucial question. And despite all the efforts to make it look rational, one is very often at a loss to explain the attitude of France in this affair. It is so strange that one sometimes wonders whether France may have misjudged the determination of its cronies in the interim government to take the atrocities to the ultimate extreme. It was all the more difficult to anticipate the extent of these killings since due to the constant news about massacres in Rwanda, the whole world had stopped paying them any attention after 1959. And so it happened that tens, or even hundreds of thousands of Tutsis were eliminated in Rwanda without much of a reaction from the rest of the globe. Bertrand Russell – the same man who was on the Tribunal against the Vietnam War – was one of the few who has spoken, from 1963 onwards, about genocide. In 1994, the strategists of the Elysée, the Quai d'Orsay and other, more discreet locations, managed to present a picture of low-key massacres which would spark off a few cries of indignation without really shocking anybody. At the end of the day, it became clear that these strategists were dangerous sorcerer's apprentices. Surely it was they and not the ageing, embittered François Mitterrand, already sick and full of contempt for his African puppets, who could have stopped the infernal machinations in time.

When the first accusations against their government became public, many French citizens reacted either with anger or a simple shrug of the shoulders. Only very few of them were prepared to admit that their country was embroiled at all in Rwanda. Today, it seems that there is a slight change of attitude. One has the impression that even in the highest government circles, some of those who were actively involved at the time are now sometimes tempted to pursue a different, slightly less delusional line of defence. For instance, the former Prime Minister Alain Juppé,[51] explaining himself on Radio France Internationale in April 2004, felt obliged to admit, with undeniable embarrassment: "We probably share some of the responsibility, just like everyone else… No more than everybody else". And regarding the story – told by Patrick de Saint-Exupéry[52] – about the French officer who burst into tears at Bisesero when he realized he had been training ruthless child killers rather than soldiers, he added: "I categorically contest that either France, or the French authorities, condoned this sort of thing [the training of militiamen] in any way whatsoever. That some soldiers may have gone astray is of course possible."

Since making a confession would be unthinkable, you admit a few mistakes and move on. At least we have progressed from the "we-are-totally-innocent" type statement, uttered with indignation, to a certain level of contrition, tempered by phrases like: "we are not the only guilty ones." Their difficulties are understandable. Quite a number of French political leaders know, sometimes down to the smallest detail, what the man in the street does not: their country went much too far in Rwanda. And they also know that the whole world is aware of it.

At the beginning of the same programme on RFI, the journalist had asked Alain Juppé, "Why is it that France hasn't managed to apologize for the Rwandan Genocide like Belgium did?"

Answer: "…I believe that it is up to the international community to pronounce their *mea culpa*."[53]

The manner in which the journalist formulated his question ("Why… *hasn't France managed to*") is of course quite mischievous: it points the finger at the psychological block that prevents France from apologizing for what happened in Rwanda.

The truth is that France cannot apologize because one would very quickly start talking about the civil wars in Chad, in the Congo, in Ivory Coast and also about the assassinations of UPC leaders in Cameroon, among other African countries, where through frontmen, it continues to make its presence felt, half a century after Independence. That is most probably how the term "disgrace," which appears in the title of Patrick de Saint-Exupéry's book, should be interpreted. The entire edifice known as *Françafrique*, the painstaking construction of which began under General de Gaulle, was in danger of collapsing or at least sustaining serious structural damage. And that wouldn't be good for business. As people say in Abidjan: "who is the crazy one?"

The slight change of attitude described above does not mean the issue has been understood, not by a long way. For a large majority of the French, the 1994 genocide undoubtedly remains a distant, insignificant event – which puts them perfectly in synch with their leaders. But the crucial work done by several French organizations,[54] which jointly have set up a Citizens Committee of Inquiry, is creating an atmosphere more favourable to an unprejudiced investigation of the facts. And in public debates, it happens less and less frequently that people speak up in defence of a country that should really be ashamed of itself. Today, everyone in France knows, even without trying to dig deeper, that Mitterrand and his powerful acolytes behaved extremely badly in Rwanda. This vague sentiment is enough to divert public opinion from the manipulative activities orchestrated by certain interest groups in the form of sensational "revelations" and books which bank on the ignorance or the indifference of the masses. The failure of these propaganda campaigns was foreseeable from the start: Rwanda, I repeat, was a very unusual case. One cannot halt such an unimaginable blood bath with one's arms. Unfortunately for those who were mixed up with this affair, people will talk about it for a long time to come. As early as April 1998, Jacques Julliard suggested in one of his columns in the *Nouvel Observateur* that sooner or later, French society would have to come clean on this issue. Emphasizing, quite rightly, the personal role of the French President, he wrote: "It is clear that we will one day have to face the question of the responsibility of France in the 1994 Genocide of the Tutsis of Rwanda, while François Mitterrand was President of the Republic. France may not have committed the crime, but France put weapons in the hands of future killers who made no secret of their intentions. In those two instances – I am sure there are others – I see no evidence that the memory of the shame of Vichy has taught us a lesson. But if we can learn anything from history at all, then it must be that the examples we can find there are all useless as long as we are not vigilant at every moment."

In fact, history takes its time, here more than anywhere else. Rwanda is such a small country, but from now on, its name will forever be associated with this extremely unusual event which strikes one as absolutely unique: a genocide. But the way we remember genocide is paradoxical; the more time passes, the less one forgets. A crime committed by the fathers is always redeemed by the sons – morally at least. Another question, very closely linked to the previous one, concerns the responsibility of the whole continent.

In Africa and also in the West, you constantly have to be prepared that someone will scoff at you and say, with a malicious glint in his eye, "Sir, you are criticizing the UN, the USA and France. Why don't you tell us a little bit about what the Africans themselves are doing about it?" And that, yes that is the very question that wakes up everybody! One can tell immediately from the rustling in the audience and the way everyone is looking for signs of irritation or embarrassment on your face. This question is usually infused with acrimony, but nevertheless tends to come from well-meaning ladies and gentlemen who are simply keen to examine these atrocities from every angle. Above all, it is an expression of their distress. Strange as it may seem, but for you, the African writer, their expectations can be summed up as follows: denigrate Africa, and most importantly, don't forget, please, to do it in French. While they are perfectly prepared to take pity on the poor Africans and even to drop them a coin or two, they refuse to feel guilty in any manner or form. The problem with a certain type of Western audience is that they are used to seeing African intellectuals who, in their desire to make money by any means possible, will present a totally undifferentiated picture of what is going on in their countries of origin. The way these countries are described makes them look oppressive and so cruel that one might think all we do even in everyday life is hate each other. And some fiction writers also use these confabulations as their stock-in-trade: "Ladies and Gentlemen, the cannibalism which is practised in my country is worse than anything you can imagine. I am going to tell you about it, even if the other Africans, those who want to conceal the true face of Africa, will accuse me of treason, but this is the sad reality." And then they start telling their fairy tales, and you might think they will never shut up. Those who listen to such stories perhaps don't always believe every word, but what actually matters to these people is that they can feel good about themselves. And it all sounds so plausible, anyway: countries where you have children for lunch and old men for supper, oh well, if there's a genocide down there, what's so amazing about that?

Conclusion: "They are saying it themselves, they are a blood-thirsty lot where they come from; Africa is really a bit different."

But actually, no: it's not different at all. If one really insisted on laying the blame for the Rwandan Genocide on *all* the Africans, then one would also have to hold the *Europeans* responsible for the Shoah and the *Asians* for the Cambodian Genocide. Why wouldn't we dare to do that in the two latter cases? Because it would be total nonsense, as everyone will easily admit. Who would dare to suggest that the Germans, as an indistinct mass of individuals, are accountable for the Holocaust? Not many people would swallow such an outrageous claim. So why does something which is so obviously absurd with regard to the others, seem to be cast in stone and basically not up for discussion when it comes to Africa? Certainly, we have cause here to be taken aback. I thought I had at least started to find an answer to this haunting question in a town in western France in January 2005, at a celebration of the liberation of Auschwitz. The organizers felt it would be a good idea to talk about the other genocides of the 20th century as well, but at the same time, it would have been out of place on that occasion to dwell on the role France had played in Rwanda. This is a pity, since it always seems a useful opportunity to me to raise this topic in front of an audience in the Hexagon. So I restricted myself to pointing out a few similarities between the destruction of the Jews of Europe and the Rwandan Genocide. But my carefully chosen words failed to make the intended impression. One gentleman, with the obvious approval of many others, made the embarrassed observation that the two events could simply not be compared, because what had happened to Rwanda… "Well… Africa, as you know perfectly well yourself…"

I presume that he didn't want to offend me – I actually remember this man as a decent chap, very sincere – and therefore didn't manage to express what he was really thinking. But it was crystal clear anyway: Rwanda simply stands for whatever you want ('massacres', 'mass murder', 'tribal warfare', 'ethnic killings') but *not genocide.* What goes on in the head of such a man, one wonders, trapped as he is in a world of pathetic and deeply inhuman prejudice without even being aware of it? It's difficult to say. Just one thing was clear:

bringing up Rwanda when we were talking about gas chambers just didn't seem right to him. This type of denial and the theory of the double genocide are the two sides of the same coin – both highlight a cultural trait that is supposedly typically African. Is it, then, so difficult to admit that the genocide of 1994 was the work of well known Rwandan politicians, strongly supported by identified French politicians? If we are talking about the latter, it is not in order to make them share the blame at all costs. But one has to point out that these non-Africans were running Rwanda, which was anything but an independent country. Today, we all know very well what that means and to claim the opposite would be misleading the entire world. This issue, as we have seen, concerns two States and not two peoples and even less two races. What the French civil society initiatives want to achieve is to put an end to the confusion. *Survie*, as well as the three other associations which were founded at the same time for the purpose of setting up a Citizens Commission of Inquiry, criticize the French government and not the French people. So it is no different from the 'not in my name' of the American opponents to Bush's infamous war in Iraq. How can one refuse to join their cause? We all know it: governments – especially the most powerful ones – often commit all sorts of atrocities far from their own borders in the name of, but unbeknown to, those who put them into power. The refusal to confront this unpleasant reality means pushing patriotism a little bit too far. It also means, in the case of Rwanda, allowing people who are certifiably mad and hatch the most dangerous plots, to pull the wool over one's eyes. It is commendable that the Citizens Commission of Inquiry formulates the problem in such a way that it is based on universal political concepts and not on an alleged culture of violence unique to Africa. It is not the first time in the history of mankind that political elites have interfered with people who wanted nothing but to be allowed to live in peace. Almost thirteen years after the genocide, can we say that we have really learnt a lesson and taken it to heart? Nothing is less certain, judging by the tragedies that have been hitting the continent incessantly since then and particularly considering the situation in Darfur. In order to prevent such an occurrence from repeating itself, it is essential to know as much about it as possible. Although it may be true that the word 'Rwanda' still strikes a certain chord in peoples' minds, the trace left there by the Hundred Days is perhaps not quite as profound as it should be. That is why it is so important to continue talking about it. The simple and straightforward act of telling the tale of a genocide – even if it is in a completely neutral manner – is in itself a recognition of the human dignity of the victims and as such a method of prevention. The ambiguities feeding on ignorance suit above all the aims of the revisionists. And the duty to remember can also mean no more than the plain reconstruction of the facts. Luckily, there are historians whose research is focused on this very topic. Over the past few years, thousands of tomes have been published on the subject, including some of a very high degree of accuracy. But it all revolves around an immense tragedy on the African continent and the problem is that very few of those texts were written by Africans.[55] If the journalists and academics of a country are so indifferent towards this genocide, one can guess that it would be worse in the rest of the population. The reaction of the younger generation deserves our attention. Talking to students in N'Djamena, or to high school pupils in Dakar, one is struck by their profound desire to understand. At any rate, when the author of a novel on Rwanda visits them in their classroom, there is nothing fortuitous about it. We go there because their teacher has made the decision on their behalf. It is important for him that they should know about the subject and he has prepared them well. These are precious moments. The clarification we can bring through our work, however modest, can have far-reaching consequences. But the bell always rings too soon and so many questions remain unanswered when it is time to leave that one wonders whether one has achieved one's goal. What stands out in the pupils' memory after the end of the discussion is the account of the most shocking atrocities and that's quite normal at that age.

But then we ask ourselves whether we have actually managed to make them understand that Rwanda was a certain moment in the history of a country and not just added proof that Africa is a basket case. They all come to class having read and annotated extracts of Primo Levi or Robert Antelme, but some of them have an unmistakable look in their eyes. They don't want to know anything, because they feel disgusted. They are so firmly on the side of the victims that any sort of discussion seems suspect to them. And for several days afterwards, we will have to live with the uncomfortable feeling of having played the devil's advocate. Since they are so used to thinking about Africa as a whole, these young people cannot make the distinction between the political and intellectual elites and the other segments of society. For them, Africa is the superfluous continent, the only one where since the dawn of time, everything has always taken a turn for the worse. This is a toxic burden to be saddled with but oddly enough, it doesn't rule out an aggressive vindication of their Africanness. The same mouth which has subjected the black race to all the moaning and groaning, may, the next minute, declare that *black is beautiful.* This is a situation where one is at a loss whether to call it mental confusion or simply disappointed love. However, I did feel rather bewildered one day when an adolescent from Bamako was talking to me about the 'primitive mentality' of the Africans. He did it very calmly, *en passant*, as it were, and as though it was something which everybody knows anyway and which is completely beyond question. Now, what was the most perplexing thing about this? The fact that he was so genuine or that it was precisely these two words which tripped off his tongue, probably by mistake? And was it really by mistake? Some useless teacher might well have planted these ideas in his head. Or perhaps he was simply happy to just listen to the adults around him. In fact, one just has to prick up one's ears to find out to what extent the popular form of Afro-pessimism – one doesn't dare call it spontaneous – has infiltrated our every day language. You can't miss all the far-fetched hypotheses and the tendency to exaggerate. Are you fed up with having to queue so long at the bank? The immediate reaction is an indignant and unequivocal: 'that's Africa, what do you expect?' which invariably receives a lot of noisy approval from bystanders. And it makes no difference whether this scene takes place in Gaborone or in Matadi – all the banks on the continent have the reputation of torturing their unfortunate clients to the point of despair. The tension rises, people start talking and there is a good chance that one will get to hear that in the West – or in Asia, for that matter – the banks are all perfect little marvels with employees who are models of exquisite courtesy. But make no mistake: the people who are saying these things only do so out of exasperation. The moment they have their money in their pocket, these philosophical convictions will dissipate until the next moment of irritation. But the question is not whether these worthy citizens have said what they really think. One would rather like to know why their exasperation always takes this particular form. Whether you praise or whether you criticize Africa, it will always be by comparison to others and never by taking into account specific situations. How is it possible for a young person who has grown up in this psychological climate not to feel disorientated? The schools, the media, the family – their common goal is to dissolve the uniqueness of his way of seeing things into a purely defensive 'we'. Unless he has a great capacity for resistance or very formative personal experiences, he will have a lot of problems in knowing who he really is. The result is utterly depressing. Whether we like it or not, half a century after what was in theory the end of the colonial era, the African elites are still fascinated by their former masters. Since they now wield the political power in our countries, it is hardly difficult for them to drag those into the wrong direction who, as the novelist Cheik Aliou Ndao has said so aptly, 'have not had the bad luck of having gone to a [French] school.' Such a frame of mind is bound to have an effect on the way each one of us interprets the most lamentable aspects of the African reality. And so it is not really surprising to find a large number of African intellectuals making comments about the Rwandan Genocide that are more or less identical to those of the most fervent racists. Self-hatred, which goes far back in our history, contributes to this attitude, but it doesn't explain everything. It is quite possible that our most basic problem is one of information. In other words: what do we know about what is *really* going on in each one of our different nations or even in the countries right next to us? Due to its painful past, Africa, which of course has the right to think of itself as one coherent block, is also in a certain way the continent of the most remote places. But more than anywhere else, this remoteness is in the mind. Someone from Senegal knows almost nothing about the political situation in Guinea-Bissau. So don't try to talk to a Ghanaian about Niger… It is more the *status quo* – with its communication problems, a triple Berlin Wall of colonial languages, etc. than a deliberate choice, but it weighs heavily upon our destiny and on the geography of our minds. Is there a civil war breaking out near us? It always seems as though these calamities appear on our borders out of nowhere, sometimes in places that are so remote and barbarian that the locals speak English or Portuguese. At the beginning of these conflicts, we hear about furious battles, but we only notice faint and disconcerting rumblings as when a thunderstorm is brewing. Then, one or two weeks later, the name of some arbitrary country starts cropping up every day during the last fifteen minutes of the television news. Liberia for example. Liberia is in flames. One reads dispatches about peace talks, about villagers being massacred in the southwest and about a humanitarian disaster. The oval unshaven face of a certain Charles Taylor is everywhere: with his red eyes and brutish appearance, this gigantic troublemaker is a sort of caricature of a 1930s gangster, especially when he is pictured wearing his famous big black sunglasses. A real bastard, this Taylor guy. He does not even stop short of sending child-soldiers to the slaughterhouse. His *lil' boyz,* as he calls them shamelessly. But beyond the fact that Liberia is on fire, beyond the atrocities that are being committed, what is *really* happening in Liberia? *What are the reasons why* a civil war is raging there? What is it *actually* that is devastating so many cities and forcing so many hundreds of thousands of people into exodus? *Who is selling the arms* to the different warlords? What about *the movers and shakers one doesn't see,* who are not even in Liberia?

Apart from the Liberians themselves, there are not many people who would be able to answer these questions, as well as some other equally simple ones. And then, one day, peace returns to Liberia. Taylor is in 5-star exile in Nigeria, but he is not going to get away with it. Soon there will be a humiliating court case at The Hague, followed by life imprisonment. Mrs. Ellen Johnson-Sirleaf duly defeated the soccer player George Weah, aka Mister George. The new lady-President took the oath and everything went smoothly with lots of democratic emotion and so on. So yesterday Liberia was at war, today Liberia is at peace. It was nothing but a bush fire. The bush fire started and now it's over. It might flare up again. In neighbouring Sierra Leone. In Uganda. In Congo-Brazaville. In Somalia. And even – why not? – all over again in Liberia.

It is so much easier to forget what happened when hardly anybody ever knew anything about it.

If we all agreed to have our conscience examined, each one of us would become aware of this deficiency, which is abnormal, to put it mildly. Decades of suffering and destruction in Zimbabwe, in Mozambique, in Angola, in the Horn of Africa and elsewhere, have failed to be inscribed in our collective memory.[56]

None of the events in these countries should have left us indifferent, but one almost feels tempted to say that millions of people lost their lives for nothing. One also has to consider that – like in Darfur – the destiny of several generations of Africans is caught up in each one of these recent tragedies and that even populations outside the war zone are affected. Isn't it strange that one does not find any articles on the recent elections in the Democratic Republic of Congo in our newspapers really scrutinizing what is at stake there economically and in terms of sovereignty. Even the fact that this ballot was so closely monitored by Brussels did not seem to arouse any suspicions. Is nobody even a bit surprised that the European Union should show more interest in the future of the former Zaïre than the African Union? In the world as it is today, this is unfortunately only to be expected. After Kosovo and Afghanistan, this is one of the rare occasions since the end of the Second World War where the Germans have actually deployed troops outside their borders and it is the first time that they have agreed to take on the command of other European forces. The political symbolism here is very important.

Who would seriously claim with a straight face that this is only to ensure that a country in central Africa sticks to the rules of the democratic game? Surely not even a complete cretin could think like that.

The point here is not that all Africans are expected to be familiar with the secret reasons behind every crisis, but one must be entitled to hope that they should have a modicum of information. Right now, this is simply not the case. Clearly, one cannot make demands of the private African press that it cannot fulfill. It has grown so fast, particularly in certain parts of the continent, that one forgets that it is still in a fledgling state and lacks financial backing. At this point of its development, it is quite normal that its focus should be on the political life of each separate country. But there are signs that private radio stations are trying harder and harder to provide greater coverage of African current affairs. West Africa Democracy Radio (WADR),[57] recently launched in Dakar, exclusively broadcasts African news programmes in both English and French.

But nothing like this existed at the time of the Rwandan Genocide. It would suffice to re-read the headlines of the Senegalese newspapers – just to mention this one example – between April and July 1994, to get an idea of the extraordinary discrepancy between the political reality on the continent as a whole and the priorities of the opinion-leaders in any one of its countries. The following anecdote, which I heard from one of the key figures, is quite telling.

A number of Rwandans living in Dakar who were surprised how indifferent the Senegalese press seemed towards the genocide at the very time it was taking place, contacted some local newspaper editors to point out this anomaly. What happened was that they were treated with great sympathy and compassion wherever they went, but that is where it ended. I remember saying to the person who told me this story years later: "Listen, if I had been in charge of a Dakar newspaper at the time, I would have done exactly the same." I then explained that I would have behaved like that not out of insensitivity, but purely due to my poor assessment of the situation. For the umpteenth civil war in a region with which Senegal was hardly familiar, the dispatches from *Agence France-Presse*, *Reuters* and *Associated Press* were quite sufficient in the opinion of the editors-in-chief. But run-of-the-mill news, even with regard to atrocities, that's not news.

This personal confession has only been repeated here for the sake of completeness and to make sure that no angle of the truth has been left in the dark. The harsh truth is, that in April and May 1994, the preparations for the Soccer World Cup were in full swing and we could not take our eyes off the American soccer fields. The African newspapers, equally preoccupied with the riveting episodes of the competition, relegated the genocide to a discreet corner of their international pages, between a train derailment in Ulan Bator and a meeting of experts of the FAO in Rome. And from one dispatch to the next, the same words cropped up again and again. Hutu. Tutsi. Who among us really knew what they meant? Very few. But what did it matter? People were furious with Henri Michel, the coach of the Cameroonian team. Getting beaten once, even badly, by Brazil, the soccer giant is OK. But 6:1 against Russia…! A proper hiding. How can anybody put those people in charge of such a stunning team? White sorcerers, if you ask me! Mercenaries, that's what they are. The fact is: we don't believe in ourselves. *What a disgrace for Africa, this Cameroonian team. We can't possibly hope for respect if we carry on like that.* And over there in Rwanda, my friend? No end in sight, they said on the news at half-time when Bulgaria was playing Greece. Yes, we are the same, aren't we? Hutu. Tutsi. A mother killed her children and the husband his wife, the teacher finished off his students with a smile and when the young man smashed the skull of his grandmother, his hands didn't even tremble…and so it continues. Rwanda. The country where love in all its forms has died a million times. Pure hatred. *A disgrace for Africa, these Rwandans. How can one earn respect with something like that?*

This attitude is quite unbearable but not necessarily wrong. It could well be some sort of survival strategy, which, whether consciously or not, takes into account the misfortunes of the Tutsis.

One can see why, in 1994, people averted their gaze from an orgy of violence so gruesome that it became surreal. Tens of thousands of bodies floating down the Nyabarongo River for days on end, that is simply too much for most normal human beings to bear. Looking at these images and trying to understand them also means accepting the risk that one might be totally crushed by a sense of shame. The shame of being African, but also the shame of belonging to the human race.

This refusal – or this fear – to know, explains rather well the deep discomfort one cannot help feeling from time to time, faced with the enormity of the Rwandan Genocide. One of my friends, whom I consider as very bright and who was never particularly impressed by the West, told me, for instance: "I have tried to understand and I have learned a certain number of things; that the terms Hutu and Tutsi have nothing to do with ethnicity and that there has never been anything resembling a genocide before the colonial era; that in the process of decolonization, Belgium created the conditions for this political mass violence; that France has armed, trained and politically supported the genocidal regime; that the international community played the role of passive accomplice." And this intellectual whose opinion reflects that of many others went on: "I know all that but I still hold the Rwandans alone responsible for what has happened in their country. OK, so they were manipulated by very powerful governments, but people who throw babies to the dogs or into bread-ovens really need to ask some questions about themselves." What he said not only commands respect because of its disarming sincerity, but it also touches a delicate issue. It is difficult to reflect on Rwanda without coming to the conclusion that it is absolutely impossible for a set of political and economic circumstances to explain such deep and utterly devastating hatred. But I found that my friend's kind of reasoning very quickly reaches its limitations. It is entirely based on the idea that the Hundred Days of Rwanda are the worst time that man has experienced on earth from the beginning until now. Even if we confine ourselves to just the 20th century, that is not the case, far from it. Wherever we are on our planet, the madness of a group of politicians will never tell us anything about the soul of a people. Besides, the words of this friend, which were mainly dictated by feelings of mortification and rage, take this debate onto such thin ice that even he would not want to risk it. If you try to push him further, he suddenly no longer knows what to say. All he can do is to grumble, "Well, it's hard to swallow that we are like that." And when I ask him, "What do you mean by being *like that?* We are like *what,* exactly? Please, try to articulate clearly what we are like and why." He looks away and instead of an answer, you get an embarrassed shrug of his shoulders. This is because we are now on the threshold of the unthinkable, quite removed from the realm where one can use language – any language – to express the darkest human feelings, in a place where words and silence frighten and carefully avoid each other. In my opinion, there is no point in walking away and repeating, with regard to the genocide of the Tutsis of Rwanda: "It's our fault," and looking as though we want to add that there is nothing new under the sun and that life has to go on. It's not true: under those circumstances, it would be death that goes on and not life.

Now, during the earliest hours of the 21st century, it is not even certain that we have so much as started to mourn the victims of the genocide. That is no doubt why others have taken it upon themselves to deliver the funeral orations in our place, in their incredibly arrogant manner. And when Jean d'Ormesson went to Rwanda for the *Figaro* in July 1994, he didn't even find it necessary to put on an act of looking anguished. Faced with hundreds of thousands of corpses scattered along the roads of a devastated country, the slightly senile academician positively quivered with delight while he was kind enough to tell his readers: "Get your handkerchiefs ready: tears will flow! This is not recommended for the squeamish: rivers of blood will flow under the blows of the machete." And without the slightest respect for the victims, whose bodies were still warm, he concluded with these utterly despicable words, "These are grandiose massacres in sublime landscapes." M. d'Ormesson's odious little phrases have no importance in themselves. But the issue that we need to ponder long and hard is that he was able to publish them in a daily newspaper with a very high print-run without receiving even a single letter of protest from the Africans in France. Only a few years ago, things would have been different. All this shows only too clearly what has become of us. Besides the "Habit of Misery" that Mongo Beti speaks about, there are other less straightforward reasons for our discretion. From the perspective of far-away Paris, the victims of this genocide are quite simply not from the right background. How can we expect negrophobic foreigners to show reverence for the dead whom we ourselves are too cowardly to mourn?

In a way, Afro-pessimism has helped the racists to get rid of all their hang-ups overnight. We certainly owe this intellectual concept a number of useful clarifications and fruitful debates, but on the other hand, it has also been used as an excuse for our spinelessness. At the end of the day, one cannot claim that the victims of the Rwandan Genocide have been vindicated. Rather, they have died twice: deprived of their lives yesterday, they have not even been granted a small memorial in our memory.

SECTION II

Beloved Country, My beautiful People!

Senegal between Cheikh Anta Diop and Léopold Sédar *Senghor*

The celebration on February 7, 2006, of the 20th anniversary of the death of Cheikh Anta Diop was followed, on October 9, by the centenary of the birth of Leopold Sedar Senghor. Hence for Senegal, 2006 was a year of great significance – such is the rivalry that continues unabated between these two great figures of our contemporary history, even long after their passing. Senghor, the first president of Senegal, always faced a relentless adversary in Cheikh Anta Diop. And the occasion was momentous indeed: an entire nation was able to take stock of its intellectual and political adventure in the 20th century. Diop and Senghor, two men of conviction, have both shaped our destiny, each one in his own way. And we have come to see the conflict between them as valuable since it can teach us so much about ourselves.

One of them was Mouride and Wolof, while the other was Catholic and Serer. We really have no choice but to acknowledge that these differences have never been properly taken into account, neither by the two men themselves, nor by their followers. Senegal as a country is 95% Muslim, but for two decades, under Senghor himself in fact, it was governed by a Catholic. His two Muslim successors took up residence in the presidential palace, one after the other with his Christian wife and it never bothered anyone.

The absence of an ethnic or religious focus in the lengthy battle between Diop and Senghor is rather surprising, considering the fact that the two men were virtually at daggers drawn at certain stages of their lives. At the beginning of the rainy season in 1962, the author of *Black Nations and Culture*[58] suffered the hardships of Diourbel prison where he spent one month in preventive detention, while Senghor was doing his utmost – applying nasty tactics at times – to prevent the dissemination of ideas whose only fault was that they differed from his own.

In fact, it seems that right from the start, life took malicious pleasure in pitting the scientist and the poet against each other.

Although his focus at the Sorbonne was the humanities, Cheikh Anta Diop was first and foremost a scientist who was schooled at the Lycée Henri IV and subsequently studied Nuclear Physics and Chemistry under Frédéric Joliot-Curie. In the minds of the African people, he remains the scholar personified, lost in deep thought, calm and austere. When he asked what could be done to "make Science flourish in Black Africa" in a text he wrote in 1975, Senghor had already made himself famous thanks to one of his most controversial utterances: "Emotion is as Black as Reason is Greek." Cheikh Anta Diop in *Black Nations and Culture* challenges this claim very fervently. Although he admits that it has an "admirable beauty," he considers it as proof of his own irreversible alienation from its author, whom he doesn't hesitate to portray as one of those "highly intellectual Blacks," who are bold enough to "actually put down in writing the fascist ideas of a presumed duality between the Black man as passionate, emotional and artistically creative and the White man as predominantly rational."

As opposed to Cheikh Anta Diop, who can be described as carved out of one block, the wavering Senghor appears rather as a man with one foot in each camp. As a Louis-le-Grand Old Boy and winner of the Agrégation de Grammaire in 1935, Senghor gives the impression that he was trying to find out his whole life who he really was. Since he could not find an answer to this question, he seems to have decided, to the point of extreme suffering and with enormous tenacity, to try to reconcile the most contradictory parts of his soul. He sang Joal and paid homage to the poetess Marone; he recited the Shaka epic better than anyone else and he wept for Martin Luther King, Jr. with a moving sincerity, saying he was "asleep, with a red rose at his throat." None of this has prevented his detractors from accusing him of putting Western culture on a pedestal. The story goes that during his two-year stint as prisoner of war, he completely baffled the guard of his *stalag* who found him reading the authors of classical antiquity in Latin and Greek. From that day onwards, they say that this German officer became his friend and took him under his wing. One might find this story a bit too heart-warming to be entirely factual and not slightly embellished, but it is just one of many anecdotes which have earned Senghor the reputation for which he is so well known. Once, he came really close to making himself the laughing stock of the Académie Française, when, while he was there and in disagreement with Jean Guitton about the definition of a certain word, he launched into a fiery refutation in… Latin, the very language in which his adversary on that particular occasion responded with equal fervour.

His colleagues must have been completely nonplussed on the one hand and delighted on the other: what better proof of the success of their civilizing mission could they wish for than this unlikely Negro-Latin classicist seen by some as "a French poet of Senegalese race?" One feels the irresistible desire, just for fun, to turn this formula on its head. How lucky that it's nonsense: until someone proves the opposite, the Senegalese will be a nation, not a race.

Senghor, the father of his country's independence – proclaimed on April 4, 1960, – quite naturally became its first head of State, a position he held for nearly a quarter of a century. Before that, from the beginning of the fifties onwards, he had been among the two or three most important political figures in the country. In his various capacities as founder of the Senegalese Democratic Party in 1948, delegate at the Palais Bourbon and Secretary of State in Edgar Faure's government, he managed to carry on his political fight and some tough philosophical battles all at the same time and without ever giving up.

As far as Cheikh Anta Diop is concerned, he started several political parties, the most important of which was undoubtedly the National Democratic Union (RND), founded on February 3, 1976. As a young man, he had distinguished himself in the student branch of the African Democratic Union (RDA), an openly anti-colonial political movement right from the day it was founded at Bamako in October 1946.

The biography written by Diop's son, Cheikh M'Backé, describes an interesting but relatively little known incident in his father's career, "Not long before the African Democratic Union was founded in 1946, Cheikh Anta Diop still believed in Léopold Sédar Senghor's intention to defend African interests, such as he, Cheikh Anta Diop, conceived them. He therefore pledged him his support during the local elections in Baol-Cayor."[59]

And this is why History could quite easily have taken a totally different course...

But Diop rid himself of this illusion, which must be attributed to his youth, very quickly. As a matter of fact, he was only just 23 years old. But at the political level, for as long as they lived, Senghor and he were destined to be the embodiment of the man of power and his opponent. The initial rift left its mark on their relationship forever. However, the various battlefields between the two rivals have never been entirely static.

This explains why the dividing lines would come close and then fade away in front of our eyes, only to reappear unexpectedly again from elsewhere, due to some particular event or another. And today, what do we actually have left of the respective legacies of Diop and Senghor in the collective memory of Senegal?

When Senghor so wisely and elegantly withdrew from power on December 13, 1980, it was by no means certain that his subjects would have been eager to keep him on. Obviously, his gesture inspired them with respect and admiration, but they must equally have felt secretly relieved. As a person, he was neither violent nor arrogant, he just used to put on a Father-of-the-Nation-type of act which came across as patronizing and off-putting. He had been in the limelight for so long that his departure could only be experienced as the start of a new era. Abdou Diouf, his successor, was certainly right when he instantly declared, "Nothing will be like it used to be." Was Senegalese society hoping for an end to the deadlock to appear out of nowhere, the sort of thing every nation wants after a political reign that has lasted too long and has therefore become a bit suffocating? The worsening economic situation, caused by the onset of a cycle of droughts in 1968, also created fresh expectations. How could it be otherwise? It is enough to mention one hugely symbolic fact: when Senghor passed the baton to Diouf, the Senegalese who were born in the year of independence had just turned twenty one, the age of legal majority. Pure coincidence? Perhaps, or else the poet secretly made a mischievous pact with chance…

Today, with hindsight, one has to say that Senghor did his best under very difficult political circumstances. His funeral and the extraordinary outpouring of emotion after his death was announced clearly demonstrated the gratitude an entire nation felt for him. One often hears people say that he governed Senegal with an unerring sense of justice and forged a modern and relatively well-organized State. This is all the more remarkable, since, throughout his time in office, he had to confront implacable adversaries. Apart from Abdoulaye Ly, Cheikh Anta Diop and Mamadou Dia, he had to contend with several other forceful ideologues and thinkers of great moral and intellectual stature. We have to remind ourselves that Senegal, where during the fifties one of the very first African communist parties south of the Sahara was founded, the African Independence Party (Parti africain de l'indépendance, PAI), has a long and sometimes downright byzantine history of ideological controversies. During the entire Senghorian era and even some time afterwards, the most obscure and enigmatic varieties of Marxism-

Leninism were flourishing there with hardly anybody knowing about it.

Senghor, who was courageous and believed in his powers of persuasion, did not hesitate to take a stand against this powerful philosophical movement. And in intellectual matters at least, more often than not, he stood almost alone against the rest of the world.

However, the history of the political repression during those years still has to be written. Senghor's police frequently subjected the militant Marxists of the PAI to savage torture and, as has been pointed out before, Cheikh Anta Diop was detained at the Diourbel prison, although not for long. From time to time, the controversy about the crisis in December 1962 reappears in the headlines and one is reminded of the unfortunate fact that the former president of the Council, Mamadou Dia, together with some of his colleagues, was sentenced to forced labour for life. They ended up spending about ten years in the Kédougou prison, which was ten years too many and based on a trial that was unfair.

One sometimes gets the impression that the Senegalese, so proud of their genteel, poetic first president, would rather not look too deeply into the darker recesses of their history. For example, nobody ever really believed the theory about the suicide of the young Maoist student Omar Blondin Diop. But who, apart from the victim's family, would still be interested in finding out the truth about what happened during that terrible night of May 13, 1971, at the prison on Gorée Island? Sadly, this story is not the only one – there are others – which one would rather not have to put on the debit side of Senghor's final balance sheet. It is largely thanks to him that Senegal enjoys the reputation of being an oasis of internal peace in the sea of death and destruction that is the rest of Africa. It is also a country where, with certain limitations, election campaigns have had a place for almost two centuries and where the army has never tried to seize power. Our good reputation is well deserved, but it must not make us forget that while Senghor was in charge, elections – the cornerstone of the legitimacy of democratic power – were neither free nor transparent. In fact, they were marred by such egregious cheating that one would rather not think about it anymore nowadays. If there had been any election observers present at the time, even the most lenient of them would have called those ballots a joke. Every citizen was at liberty to start a political party or –association, but unless they were pro-government, such organizations did not really have a chance to pursue their objectives. They were kept under close surveillance, were not allowed to act or even be visible, since the media were under the absolute control of the State. Semantic cover-ups like 'united party' or 'dominant party' have long served the purpose of masking a far less attractive reality: we were living in a *de facto* one-party State that was greedily devouring all the institutions.

The Senghorian *modus operandi* can hardly be called elegant, but it could have been so much worse. It is true that he was less democratic than he appeared to be, but he certainly never spread an atmosphere of terror in the country. Everyone was allowed to express his opinion freely and publicly without risking a visit from the security police. Senghor always stayed away from heavy-handed, brutal oppression both because it was foreign to his temperament and out of prudence. As a politician, he would probably have subscribed to the distinction, made by a well-known humourist, between dictatorship and democracy: the former, he said, means "Shut up!" and the latter, "Oh really? That's fascinating…"

The Senegalese President clearly understood that it was better to gag his opponents than to turn them into martyrs. Then they could talk as much as they liked, but nobody could hear them anymore. And when they realized they were fighting a losing battle, many of them ended up becoming his allies. Invariably when this happened, he, magnanimous ruler that he was, would welcome them with open arms, and instead of treating them with contempt, showed them great consideration.

Since this is supposed to be a comparison between the two men, it is important to stress that Cheikh Anta Diop was one of the few important political leaders to have refused him this pleasure. And this is not for lack of trying on the part of Senghor. Diop made interesting revelations about the regime's attempts to get closer to him in a key text published in 1979 in *Taxaw*, the newspaper owned by his party, the National Democratic Union (RND). The following is an example: "In 1963, after Mamadou Dia, the president of the cabinet, had left, Senghor entered into negotiations with the BMS (Bloc of the Senegalese Masses), which at the time was threatening to destabilize the regime. He offered us 5 ministerial posts (2 full ministries and 3 positions for Secretaries of State, including the one for Foreign Affairs, which would be set up if we came to an agreement), and a quarter of the deputies in the National Assembly, which meant initially 13 deputies, but 20 after the split from the PRA (African Union Party). This offer came with one non-negotiable condition: the BMS had to be closed down." Diop refused to get in on the act of this horse-trading, which he found distasteful. In order to tempt him, Senghor, clever as always, casually let slip, "Once I see that I can trust you, you can do whatever you want." But he failed. What Senghor's enticing offers did do, however, was to create a division in Cheikh Anta Diop's party, with the result that some of the executive members abandoned their leader. The government disbanded the BMS and Diop immediately started another political group, the Senegalese National Front (FNS). Senghor tried again. He was absolutely determined to win Cheikh Anta Diop over, and only him. But Diop was not interested in his new propositions, with the result that the FNS never became officially accredited. Thirteen years later, in 1976, Diop founded the National Democratic Union (RND). Not only did Senghor refuse to acknowledge this group, but he also went so far as to modify the constitution in order to limit the number of parties to four, in terms that specifically excluded the RND.

As one can see, these confrontations were frequently pretty head-on. The intellectual stature of the two men did nothing if it didn't make their relationship more tempestuous. Senghor always seems to have believed that Diop rejected him more as a human being than because of their differences of opinion. He could not stop sneering at Diop's "crypto-personal opposition" in his speeches. Even those who hardly knew Cheikh Anta Diop found the inanity of this accusation laughable. But Diop was angry and took revenge by bringing up an incident from the past which was not particularly flattering for Senghor: "In 1955, before the Overseas Reform Act was even introduced, France under the Faure Administration, to which Senghor belonged, wanted to reconsider its political ties with its African colonies. It was therefore decided that in issue 8 of the NEF, Senghor and I would write the two articles on doctrine which were bound to have a fairly profound impact on the looming reforms. At any rate, the two pieces were supposed to serve as reference material. Despite the obvious urgency of this matter, but with the backing of the students of the RDA at the time, I refused to deliver the requested text, because that would have come down to my sanctioning reforms which could, in the short term at least, only be neo-colonial in content: should this be described as crypto-personal antagonism or were we dealing with differing ideological convictions here? To this day, it is the neo-colonialist essence of Senghor's regime that is the problem and not the man."[60]

In the end, the outcome was embarrassing to say the least. Senghor, unable to 'appease' Cheikh Anta Diop by granting him material benefits, systematically disbanded or refused to recognize the political parties he started. This is why it is indeed questionable whether, in those early days, Senegal really was a *democratic exception* which is what everyone likes to call it. Perhaps it would be more accurate to talk about the *Senegalese paradox*: a political system which pretended to be pluralist but wasn't, which was cynical about universal suffrage, but generously authorized freedom of speech.

This anomaly is, in a way, our family secret. Today, it seems that our politicians, some of whom have suffered greatly under Senghor's regime, would rather forget about their ordeal in order to preserve this perfect picture. There is, for example, the case of one of Senghor's fierce former adversaries who claimed with great sincerity that in historical terms, the poet-president had shown himself far more perceptive about the big issues of our time than his opponents of the far left, among many others. And this, interestingly enough, happened not long before Senghor's death. This forgiving attitude may well have been reinforced by comparisons which were rather flattering for Senegal: during those leaden years the Spaniard Francisco Franco, Antonio Salazar from Portugal, the Zaïrean Mobutu Sese Seko, François Duvalier, aka Papa Doc from Haïti, the Chilean Augusto Pinochet and a whole crowd of Latin American generals appointed by the CIA, were committing human rights violations of a far more serious nature. Besides, one can be certain that the Senegalese politicians, all of whom had a great deal of experience, were very well aware at which point power, especially in a poor country under foreign domination, can open the floodgates to senseless violence. Senghor had the strength to keep them closed.

Senghor's poetic work has frequently been under the spotlight in recent months. Nobody will want to complain about the tributes he has received from around the world. His country knows and appreciates how much it owes him, but it doesn't stand still. It is not that surprising then that a few jarring notes are occasionally heard in Senegal spoiling the collective praise singing. While we can't really blame a non-fiction writer from Ivory Coast or a Belgian novelist for seeing in Senghor purely the admirable literary figure that he was, a Senegalese intellectual will find it rather more difficult to keep quiet about the other facets of his personality. Some very recent memories forbid it. Wouldn't it be nice if all a head of government had to do in order to eschew taking responsibility for his choices and political decisions, was to compose some great poetry? This man held our destiny in his hands and it is our duty to ask ourselves what he did with it. If we don't, our children and our children's children will miss out on an essential part of their own history. And after all those years of bashful silence about the Senghorean era, it will do us all good to revisit what has been repressed. An entire generation – mine, in fact – has been at loggerheads with him to the extent that we sometimes wanted to hate him, although we knew that beyond his questionable political choices, he was an intellectual worthy of respect. There were times when one couldn't help feeling a strange sort of affection for him. Retracing his trajectory is a way, for some of us, of settling a few accounts from our youth. The question secretly tormenting everybody's conscience today is what we really truly think of Léopold Sédar Senghor. It is a very personal battle and one feels in danger of being swept away by a tide of feelings that are difficult to control.

So what does it mean, 2006, the Senghor year? One could try, if this is such a perfect opportunity to revisit our Senghor years, to stick to his own favourite formula: "with neither unnecessary cruelty nor reprehensible weakness." It is perhaps too soon to pass a dispassionate judgment on the politician and his legacy.

But looking back over the few years which have passed since then, we can ask ourselves whether Senghor was Senegal's protection against despotism and dictatorship – nobody knows the answer to that, of course. It is just that, even if a lot of what he did was good for us, one hesitates to call him the best president we could have had at that point in history. No, we are not talking about a choice between Senghor and Bokassa. There must have been some other alternatives to his regime than one of those grotesque "revolutions" which brought quite a number of countries to their knees. But, be that as it may, Senegal was lucky to have gained its independence under the stewardship of Senghor and not some appallingly sadistic monster.

There are certain commentators today who have come up with subtle theoretical variations on this theme: Senghor the presidential poet or the poet-president? The bets are still open, although not many seem to consider this as a particularly burning question. One thing is certain though, and that is that Senghor never hesitated to use his eminent social position to further his literary career. Throughout the period while he was in power, both his closest party political confidants and his regional administrators in the most remote corners of the country seemed to feel compelled to hold forth at length on topics like the Asymmetrical Parallelism or the spiritual path of Father Pierre Teilhard de Chardin and the result was mostly utter garbage, to be honest. The fact is that in Senegal, nobody really gave a tinker's curse about Father Teilhard de Chardin… no one had the faintest idea who he was and why it was so important to talk about him all the time. But so what? We saw no reason to stop talking about the honourable Father Teilhard de Chardin and so we carried on. Would it be possible to dream up a more…surreal situation for a newly independent African country?[61] On the other hand, one has the impression that Senghor played the role of the official court poet at his own court, declaiming and then explaining his verses in front of his minions who were pretty much forced to enjoy the spectacle. All this was of course totally useless, since the idea of turning *négritude* into the national ideology did not work out as expected. From the moment when he withdrew from public life, the terms *African socialism* and *négritude* ceased to be *en vogue* and are only rarely heard today. It is not impossible that late in life, the man felt somehow disillusioned, after never having missed the slightest opportunity of forging his image as a thinker with penetrating, even prophetic insights. His collection of essays entitled 'Liberty,' where he expresses his basic cultural and political ideas, highlights this ambition. What he wrote is certainly not insignificant, but one is captivated more by its stylistic elegance than its depth and coherence of thought. It may reveal Senghor's vast erudition and genuine love of his country, but what sticks in one's memory is essentially just a few nicely chiselled repetitive phrases softly murmured – sometimes lofty, at other times a bit limp. Senghor's primary merit is perhaps to have been courageous enough to stand by a frankly idealistic worldview in an era when an intellectual from the Developing World could generally only make himself heard by proclaiming platitudes about the dictatorship of the proletariat. While his opponents were predicting a bloodbath on a global scale, he, much more reasonably, was advocating the intermingling of all the peoples of the world. One may be excused for thinking that history has intervened in his favour. The idea of mixing different populations, culturally as well as biologically, is indeed becoming an option for every single human being. And it is certainly true that in its most positive aspects, our globalized world today strongly resembles what Senghor had in mind. But on closer scrutiny, one quickly understands that this idea of "Living together in Peace and Harmony" is not what the future holds: nowadays more than ever before, we are ruled by the principle that being stronger equals being better. It looks as though this attitude is taking hold of the whole of humanity and the value systems of the weaker nations will be mercilessly stamped out in the process. It is these very value systems that have been blamed for their economic backwardness. For the African, the entrance ticket to the "universal banquet" – another expression dear to Senghor's heart – is clearly too expensive: before he can do anything else, he is told to get rid of his language and his spirituality, which means his soul. This is of course not what the writer had envisaged. But sadly, it turns out that the intrigues and stratagems of the rich countries resulted in the exact opposite of the cherished dream of the humanist with the "Catholic heart."

High School students who only know him by name should know that he is the patron saint of grand elegiac poetry. In Senegal and in other African countries, everyone knows 'Black Woman' and 'Joal' by heart. Whether they are well known or totally obscure, most of the young writers from Africa South of the Sahara and especially from the francophone countries, look up to him unreservedly. The fact that a number of these writers have dedicated their books to Senghor in this centenary year proves this. What fascinates them about the author of 'Shadow Songs' and 'Nocturns,' is that the exercise of power never made him lose sight of the primacy of poetry over politics.

It is the magic of this great art form that made his encounter in Paris with Césaire from Martinique and Damas from Guyana so meaningful. It gave birth to a new way of thinking which set the entire African continent and its Diaspora on fire with an intellectual effervescence that was infectious. In the fierce battles that followed, Senghor himself received his fair share of knocks. There was a time when it was basically *de rigueur* to be passionately anti-Senghor. In retrospect, there is a danger that we only retain the most derisory aspect of the entire phenomenon of *négritude*, such as the macho swagger of a few ambitious young pseudo-intellectuals. But personalities of the calibre of Stanislas Adotevi, Pathé Diagne and Mongo Beti didn't make things so difficult for Senghor just for fun. They had very good reasons to believe that the great negro-African bard was also the most devoted – not to say obsequious– of collaborators of the former colonizers.

We are well aware that the phenomenon of *francophonie* serves the purpose of furthering France's intention to play a leading role both in Africa and in the rest of the world. Senghor was not content with being one of the founding fathers – together with the presidents Habib Bourgiba of Tunisia and Hamani Diori of Niger.[62] Thanks to his literary fame, he gave it the necessary credibility and then defended it with such unwavering loyalty that the French must have been slightly perplexed by his boundless devotion towards them.

This took such an extreme form so early on that serious doubts arose concerning his true nationality. All the former activists from the National Democratic Union (RND) remember the *question* coming up regularly on page one of every issue of *Taxaw*, the newspaper published by Cheikh Anta Diop's party. It was worded as follows: "The Senegalese people are entitled to know whether the man in charge of their administration has retired from his public duties in France at the age of 65, while continuing to be President of the Republic of Senegal and if this is the case, on what grounds he was able to do so. In other words, is Senghor, implicitly or explicitly, continuing to hold

French nationality to this day?" The man in question never replied, but the issue became the butt of many jokes in the inner circle of the RND. Whenever an activist mentioned the question, everybody immediately got the message and saw it as a chance to make all sorts of jokes about patriotism, aimed at certain leaders with a lisp who were completely sold to the foreign powers.

In his public speeches, Cheikh Anta Diop himself had used every opportunity to condemn the purely nominal independence of a country where the technical assistance of France had effectively become a 'parallel government' and represented the true centre of power, all its lackeys' derisory pretensions at sovereignty notwithstanding.

Furthermore, it is a good idea to examine another question whose answer is not as obvious as it seems: what exactly was the role Senghor played in the creation of *Françafrique*? *Françafrique* reeks of oil; it conjures up the destruction of forests by gangs of ruthless timber thieves, arms trafficking, the gambling industry, mercenaries and undercover agents who specialize in turnkey coups d'état, transfers of billions from one bank account to another inbetween hunting parties and sex orgies. Its representatives, on the African side, are stereotypes: uneducated, coarse and brutal rabble-rousers, who meekly take their orders from Paris.[63]

This profile in no way corresponds with that of Senghor, who, quite apart from anything else, was president of a country completely lacking in natural resources. As a result, he was definitely not involved in the most hideous aspects of the *françafrican* marriage: Bokassa's diamonds, the Elf trial, assassinations of political opponents, in fact all the shady dealings to do with sex, violence and money between masters and their servants who are equally corrupt.

Despite this, it is not impossible that from a strategic point of view, Senghor was more useful to *Françafrique* than the majority of his peers. As a head of State who was decent, honest and civilised in every way, he was of great assistance to the former colonial power for a very long time. Who else was there besides him who could have developed the francophone project, now so profitable that it extends its political tentacles in the most unexpected directions? In the course of a recent private conversation, a female French academic summed up the case of the author of Joal with this pithy and eminently valid formula: 'Senghor was exactly what the colonizers wanted.' The very least one can say is that he was too often unsure whether his heart was in France or in Africa. There is a passage in *A Long Walk to Freedom*[64] – Mandela's autobiography – which makes one think.

This text is definitely worth the digression.

It is the early sixties, when, on the way home after a meeting in Addis Ababa, Nelson Mandela and Oliver Tambo are secretly visiting other African capitals in order to organize arms, training camps and money for *Umkhonto we Sizwe*, the newly created militant branch of the African National Congress (ANC). William Tubman of Liberia, Julius Nyerere of Tanganyika, Sékou Touré of Guinea and Habib Bourgiba of Tunisia are some of the African leaders who are giving them a warm welcome. The Senegalese capital is, in February 1962, the last stop on their journey and this is Mandela's unabridged account of it: "The slender fishing boats gliding gracefully into the port of Dakar was only equalled by the elegance of the Senegalese women who seemed to be floating around the city dressed in undulating robes with their heads covered by a turban. I was wandering around the nearby market place with its exotic spices and intoxicating aromas. The Senegalese are a beautiful people and I very much enjoyed our brief stay in their country. This society proves how many totally disparate elements – French, Muslim and African – can intermingle and create a new, unique and distinctive culture.

On our way to meet President Leopold Senghor, Oliver suffered a severe asthma attack. He refused to return to the hotel and so I put him on my back up and carried him up the stairs to the president's office. Senghor was very concerned to see Oliver in this state and insisted that he should be seen by his personal physician.

I had been advised to be wary of Senghor, for there were reports that Senegalese soldiers were fighting alongside the French in Algeria and that he himself was a bit too taken with the customs and charms of the *ancien régime.* The emerging nations have always felt an abiding attraction to the way of life of the colonizer – myself included. President Senghor was an academic and a poet; he told us that he was collecting documentation about Shaka, flattering us by asking us a lot of questions about the great South African warrior. We gave him a description of the situation in our country and presented our request for support, both with the training of our soldiers and money. Senghor's reply was that his hands were tied until the next parliamentary session.

But he said that while we were waiting, he wanted us to talk to the minister of Justice, M. Daboussier [*sic*] about the military training and its problems and then the president introduced a very beautiful young French girl to me who, he said, would be our interpreter. I didn't say anything, but I was worried. I did not feel comfortable with the idea of discussing sensitive issues like military training in front of a young woman whom I didn't know and was not sure I could trust. Senghor sensed my unease and said: "Don't worry, Mandela, the French who live here identify completely with our specifically African problems."

But when we went to see the minister, the secretaries at the reception desk were African and one of them asked the French woman what she was doing here. She replied that the president had sent her as an interpreter. An argument ensued and one of the secretaries turned towards me and asked, "Do you speak English, Sir?" I told her that I did and she said, "The minister speaks English, so you can talk to him directly, without an interpreter." The young woman stayed there while I went to talk to the minister who promised his assistance. In the end, we did not receive from Senghor what we had asked for, but he provided me with a diplomatic passport and paid for our plane tickets from Dakar to London."[65]

Mandela does not comment on this report with a single word. And actually, would it have been necessary? Senghor's conduct speaks for itself and frankly sends a shiver down one's spine. It would of course be unfair to limit his role in the struggle against Apartheid to this extremely disturbing episode. But it would be equally wrong to pretend that this side of Senghor did not exist. We are talking about historical facts here and one cannot simply avert one's eyes when suddenly the impressive features of the author of *Shaka* are displaced by the more unsettling ones of the unscrupulous politician who is perfectly at ease in his camp… which is very clearly *not* the one of the oppressed South African people.

Senghor is buried in Dakar, in the catholic cemetery of Bel-Air, having spent the last twenty years of his life in Verson. And completely contrary to all common sense, the Senghor Foundation is also based in this little town in Normandy. When he died there, on Thursday, December 20, 2001, a very revealing dispute erupted in the media. The profound lack of interest in this event on the part of the French authorities was a shock to many people in Senegal and abroad. Thus, the writer Erik Orsenna attached his signature to an article in the French daily *Le Monde* with the headline, "I feel ashamed!"[66] There is really no need to pause and reflect on the hypocrisy of this article and some others like it. But of course this controversy was also a confession: at the time when Senegal and Africa were weeping for Senghor, it seemed obvious to the rest of the world that it should be the same everywhere in France. To accuse France of extraordinary ingratitude towards him is also an open acknowledgement that he was always at the beck and call of this foreign country. Is it possible that he did more for that country than for his native Senegal? We will never know. The fact that this is so difficult to answer is enough to demonstrate the great complexity of the man.

The difficulty intellectuals have in forming an opinion is generally not shared by the man in the street, far from it. The Senegalese people continue to see in Senghor a political leader of great humanity, who was in favour of dialogue at all costs and with everybody. Members of the older generation sometimes recall, with a tender little smile, this man with the peculiar voice who always punctuated his sentences with the same, slightly mysterious expressions: "now therefore…", *hic et nunc*, "all things considered", *homo senegalensis* etc. In the country of the Four Districts, you couldn't help admiring "the first scholar and grammarian in Africa South of the Sahara",[67] who was even more accomplished than the *Toubabs*[68] themselves in their language and their good manners.

*

Cheikh Anta Diop, a man who fought one and the same battle all his life, albeit on several fronts, was born on December 29, 1923, in Caytu, a small village in Baol about 150km east of Dakar. He was the total opposite of Senghor, in the sense that no one ever managed to detect even the slightest intellectual or political ambivalence in him. Paraphrasing Césaire, one could say about him: He was a Negro and a Negro he remained until the end. This does not mean he was dogmatic in any way. On the contrary, he was subtle and cautious, despite the contagious strength of his convictions.

Diop was only thirteen when he came to Dakar where he lived with his mother Magatte Diop in the crowded Medina, on the corner of 7th and 16th Street, to be precise, and went to the famous Lamine Guèye secondary school. This establishment, where Senghor, too, had been a student a few years earlier, was then called Van Vollenhoven, and was the most prestigious school in all of what, in those days, was known as 'French Black Africa'.

It is important to point out that Cheikh Anta Diop graduated from there in 1945, with two High School Diplomas, having passed Science in June and the Humanities in October. This is a rare feat, but not really surprising; he struck everyone who met him during that period of his life as unusually gifted. He was only in his third year when he invented an alphabet that he hoped to be able to use one day for a unified transcription of all the African languages. This did not go any further, but it is an example of his precocious ideas and his early interest in scientific research. And in 1960, he himself put its significance into perspective by saying with his customary modesty, "I worked on this research project during my third year at the Van Vollenhoven secondary school in Dakar and it was childish, I admit. I started wondering about the etymology of certain words in Wolof and was asking myself whether we couldn't perhaps have our own script. So I developed an alphabet with special characters all those years ago and submitted it to Cissé Ndiarmèw at the CFA Committee in Dakar in 1944. But I have given up on this independent writing-system since then. If M. Cissé accepted it out of paternal kindness, it was because he expected that ultimately, the research would bear fruit…[…]. I embarked on a purely scientific career. The schooling I had received may have turned me into an African with a lot of knowledge, but I lacked a rounded education. I felt as if I was in a cultural void."[69]

When he went to France in 1946 on a bursary from the Dakar Municipality, he quickly attracted the attention of the African community in Paris, partly because of his exemplary academic record and partly due to his involvement with anti-colonial organizations.

January 9, 1960 is a date of special importance in his intellectual life. It marks the day he defended his doctoral thesis on the following subject: *A Study comparing European and African Political and Social Systems, from Antiquity to the Formation of Modern Nations.* This defence was supposed to have taken place in 1954, but had had to be cancelled although the written part of the thesis was complete. His views were too diametrically opposed to the received academic opinions of the day and due to the multidisciplinary nature of the subject, it had not been possible to put together a jury. The dissertation had to be published in a rush in 1954 under the title *Black Nations and Cultures* by *Présence africaine*, a publishing house in Paris started by Alioune Diop seven years previously.

The defence of the thesis, when it eventually happened, was quite an event. Every single African student in France with a reputation for being rebellious and progressive was there. They all knew perfectly well that Cheikh Anta Diop's project represented an attack on the sacrosanct institution of French academia. The cross-examinations were stormy and abnormally long, lasting longer than six circles around the clock. Candidate Diop defended himself steadfastly on every point. He could see that the professors were just full of hot air and their habit of spreading terror all around them did not impress him in the slightest. One thing is certain: it was not an ordinary doctoral defence, since the large, noisy audience in the Louis-Liard lecture hall of the Sorbonne did not hold back its opinions, obviously all in favour of the rebel candidate.

He received no more than a merit for his work, which in the French system meant he was not authorized to teach. This was doubly outrageous, since for one thing, the Sorbonne refused to recognize the achievements of one of the most profound and prolific thinkers of his time in order to punish him, with extraordinary pettiness, for his independence of spirit. Secondly, it was Cheikh Anta Diop's most cherished wish to be able to hand on his knowledge to young Africans, but he had been refused permission to do so. Later on, President Senghor did not hesitate to throw his weight behind this iniquitous decision by a jury of the Sorbonne, thus ensuring that he was prevented from teaching at the university of Dakar in any capacity whatsoever.

But thanks to one of those ironies for which History is well known, today, this university carries his name. The same goes for the institute where Cheikh Anta Diop established a Carbon-14 research laboratory, *the Fundamental Institute of Black Africa*, or IFAN [Institut fondamental d'Afrique noire], as well as, incidentally, the longest street in Dakar, the Old Ouakam Road, which happens to run past the university! Leaving aside these posthumous tributes, it needs to be mentioned that being barred from teaching in no way dampened the pedagogical zeal of the young graduate, it rather intensified it. On the very day of his *viva voce* examination, he announced his imminent return to Senegal in the press: "I am definitely going back to Black Africa as soon as next week, where I will make every effort to contribute to the education and training of future leaders and also to the development of research, both in the social- and in the natural-sciences."[70]

He was well aware of all the other challenges awaiting him and he felt ready to take them on. Not only was he planning to fight for the genuine independence of Senegal, but also for the creation of a federation of states in Africa South of the Sahara. And as far as Africa South of the Sahara as a whole was concerned, it was his ambition to restore it to its former greatness by proving that its ancient civilization was not only the starting point, but also the centre of all human evolution.

As early as 1955, Césaire made the following comment on this powerful mind in the second edition of his *Discourse on Colonialism*: "I don't want to go into the question of what the historians, nor what the historians of colonization, nor what the Egyptologists did. What the historians did is all too obvious, while the mechanism of obfuscation in the second case has been exposed once and for all by Cheikh Anta Diop in his book: *Black Nations and Cultures* – the most courageous work by a black author to date. There is absolutely no doubt that it will play a significant role in the awakening of Africa."[71]

Unlike so many others before him, the Senegalese scholar Cheikh Anta Diop was not content with stating that Africa was never a *tabula rasa*. The so-called enlightened Western intelligentsia would have no problem with granting that much. The idea of all human civilizations being equal – in principle, why not? If a concept is formulated in such general terms, even the most vicious reactionaries can give the impression of being in agreement, while at the same time quietly imposing severe reservations on it. Diop knew that it would not be an easy task to change things. He also knew that he was attacking the most deeply rooted philosophical prejudices of his time and that he would have to do more than entrance the world with his incantations. In retrospect, one cannot but marvel at his clear-sighted boldness. We are neither dealing with an isolated case of lunacy here, nor with gratuitous claims: Cheikh Anta Diop introduced arguments of great scientific value and was thus able to underpin what other African intellectuals had said before, but on a purely emotional basis.

Western Egyptologists were quick to marginalize him and occasionally they were even rude enough to refuse to acknowledge the existence of his work altogether. But Cheikh Anta Diop and a growing number of scientists across the world who supported his ideas continued to plough their furrow. The majority of his followers consisted of black African intellectuals and black members of the diaspora. Cheikh Anta Diop's adversaries, on the other hand, have often been suspected of being racially prejudiced and hence refusing the mere suggestion that black civilizations may have played a predominant role in the history of mankind. The result is a situation more conducive to ideological bickering than to calm, rational debate. Diop was always wary of a narrowly political interpretation of his work, because he knew that that was precisely what the sceptics of all different hues wanted. Instead he always made a point of discussing the archaeological and historical evidence with his peers. And when UNESCO requested his assistance with the publication of the Africa volume of *The General History of Mankind*, he accepted on condition that a high level meeting should be held during which all the Egyptologists alive at the time would be asked to report their findings. UNESCO complied with his wish and organized a symposium in Cairo from January 28 to February 3, 1974, on the topic, "The population of ancient Egypt and the decipherment of the Meroïtic script." This intellectual challenge by Diop and the Congolese Théophile Obenga left their Western colleagues stumped. By holding on to their opinions without being able to disprove the factual evidence in front of them, they basically admitted that they had been blinded by cultural and racial prejudice. Although Diop and Obenga realized that far more was at stake than their personal pride, courtesy reigned during the debates, which were conducted in the disciplined manner one would expect from scientists. At the end of six days of mutual exchange, it was clear that they and their views had won the upper hand.

The official report on the Cairo Symposium leaves no doubt about this. Cheikh Anta Diop's biographer has summed it up as follows:

"The Cairo Symposium marks a huge step forward in African historiography, the writing of the history of Africa. For the first time and under the aegis of UNESCO, African academics have had the opportunity to compare their findings in the field of Egyptology with those of their counterparts in other countries. The participants [...] were impressed by the multidisciplinary research methodology pioneered by Cheikh Anta Diop and Théophile Obenga [...]. The recommendations at the end of the symposium stress the solidity of the arguments presented by the two Africans in their lectures and during the debates and they explain the scientific progress they should bring about. Although the ethnic composition of ancient Egypt continues to be controversial, it has been unanimously accepted that linguistically and in general cultural terms, pharaonic Egypt belonged to the Negro-African world. The Egyptologist Serge Sauneron in particular (he was killed in an accident a few years after the Cairo symposium), a great expert in the Egyptian language and grammar who inspired the re-publication of the impressive catalogue of the hieroglyphic script by the French Institute of Oriental Archaeology, recognized that ancient Egyptian is not related to the Semitic languages. He approved of Cheikh Anta Diop and Théophile Obenga's research method and he emphasized the great significance of their work in comparative linguistics."[72]

It is not really surprising that by 1966, together with the African American W.E.B. Du Bois, Diop had already attracted attention as a writer whose oeuvre had an enormous influence on Black intellectuals of the 20th century and their thinking. He was only forty-two years old... One also needs to remember that Cheikh Anta Diop was publicly honoured, even in Senegal, on the occasion of the World Festival of Negro Art under the patronage of President Senghor. Yet another example of the complex relationship between the two men. But despite these small exceptions, the francophile Senghor and the anti-colonial Diop never really saw eye to eye on the essential issues.

Their antagonism came to a head when on February 3, 1976, Diop founded the National Democratic Union (RND). For several years after that, political life in Senegal seemed to revolve around Senghor's attempts to deprive Diop of this last chance of expressing himself in an organised setting. The govern–ment eventually used the excuse that…grammatical rules (!) had been breached, in order to be able to ban *Siggi*, the party-political newspaper of the RND.[73]

The history of the RND remains to be written. Cheikh Anta Diop had hoped to formulate its party manifesto and keep it going in perpetuity. Perhaps one has to see here above all the desire to define his territory more clearly after the less fortunate attempts with the 'Union of the Senegalese Masses' and the 'Senegalese National Front.'

While being a political party in the traditional sense, the RND also had the ambition to revolutionize political practices. Both internally and in their dealings with the public, the party leaders were extremely conscious of ethical issues and felt, with good reason, that they were atypical. For Diop, it was also a means of bridging the gap between the intellectual elites and the masses of the Senegalese working- and peasant-class. In actual fact, the RND turned out to be more a peasant party than a workers' organization. Cheikh Anta Diop himself was the interface between them, a role which suited him admirably. He genuinely belonged to both of these worlds and he wanted to create a synergy between them. He was a simple man whom one could never imagine wearing a tailcoat or, as the poet David Diop put it, "holding forth in the drawing rooms of condescension." Although he came to Dakar when he was very young, in some way, he never left Baol where he was born. Unlike Senghor, he always remained, with every fibre of his being, a product of his native territory. He was intimately familiar with the vernacular version of Wolof as it is spoken in the rural areas and he frequently, in both private and public political meetings, insisted on talking exactly like someone who has never set foot in a French school… And he was better than anyone at slotting into a group with just a single sentence. This, for example, is how he made fun of a 'national' assembly where it was forbidden to speak the national languages, "*La ñuy wax ca péncum réew ma, su ma leen ko tekkiloon tey jii ci wolof, ngeen gàdduy yat dàqileen!*"[74] After a good laugh, the crowd started to mull over the seriousness of what this highly unusual 'politician', affectionately called 'Cheikh' by everyone had just said. He had forced them to recall one of his leading principles which was that trying to persuade the people that development and democracy can be promoted in a foreign language is deception. Wherever he went, he used to immediately address those on the periphery: "You are excluded from the debate on your future by the imposition of a language which is only understood by a small minority. Don't be intimidated by these long words; it is no secret what these people are saying and that it is both stupid and harmful to our nation!"

His other persona was that of the teacher, trying to show how hard it is to reconcile ethics and politics in a country which is not sure of itself: "*Nit ñi dañ leen a na nax ba soo leen waxee dëgg sax tas seen yaakaar!*"[75]

There are an infinite number of similar examples. At times like these, his keen desire to speak the truth and nothing but the truth, was even more conspicuous than usual. From the moment when he abandoned French in favour of Wolof, his diction, just like his facial expression and his gestures changed. It was a surprise to find that this scholarly man had a very personal style and a penchant for elaborate little sentences, spiked with lethal innuendoes. Cheikh Anta Diop had nothing in common with the usual run-of-the-mill politicians who find it an ordeal having to express themselves in their mother tongue and who will only do it out of fake solidarity with the people for the duration of the meeting.[76]

It was he more than anyone else, who had the courage and persistence to expose the system of neo-colonial domination embodied by Senghor. This is why Cheikh Anta Diop had no difficulty in gathering a significant number of Senegalese left-wing intellectuals around him, including several, still beardless, former activists left over from the student protests who at one time had seriously hoped to be able to besiege the cities with the help of the rural population.

Towards the end of his life and namely after Senghor's retirement, Diop lost some of his political influence and the RND, weakened by internal discord, began to show its limitations. Its concept, however, had been very promising and the party existed long enough to seriously worry the regime. Senghor, with the help of his French advisers, took it upon himself to dream up the despicable laws that allowed him to ban it. But if the RND was conceived with the intention of making it an enduring and powerful political force, one has to say that the end-result has not borne out the early expectations. Its legacy is also sadly divided. Right now, in our political camp, there simply is no such thing as a coherent body of thought which could be attributed to Cheikh Anta Diop. However, more and more interesting personalities in a variety of cultural sectors and organizations are feeling an affinity with his struggles and admire in him the man and the intellectual. This does not change the fact that the parties, which were direct offshoots of the original RND, remained political lightweights and failed to make up for this by building a vigorous critical presence. Two focal points in Cheikh Anta Diop's political mission – the battle against neo-colonialism and the promotion of African languages – have definitely been totally marginalized in the national debate. Their quasi-disappearance in such a short time is difficult to explain. Is it because, against all evidence, those issues are considered solved and thus no longer relevant? Or is it as a result of guerrilla warfare, a permanent political force these days, which doesn't leave anybody at leisure to think further ahead into the future? Whatever the reason, one fact seems obvious and that is that the majority of our political leaders, no matter whether they belong to the ruling party or the opposition, would just chuckle if one presented them with these questions. The Senegalese intellectual of today seems to be more in tune with the Senghorian model than with Cheikh Anta Diop's slightly desperate dreams. Does that mean we have to call Diop a failure? That would probably be going too far, since Senegalese society is full of other forces whose power is difficult to gauge and which may, at the end of the day, turn out to be more effective than anything else. But one can sometimes not help feeling that Senghor has modified our mental attitude much more profoundly than we care to admit.

In retrospect, one has the impression that soon after Senghor's withdrawal from power, Diop's scientific work started to gain the upper hand over his immediate political preoccupations. Is this mere coincidence? *Prima facie*, one cannot rule it out.

But it is also possible that at that point, Diop wanted to put some distance between himself and the new generation of decision-makers, or indeed, he may have sensed that the end of his life was approaching. It remains a fact that some of his most memorable conferences took place between 1982 and his death in 1986. He went to London, Niamey, Algiers, Pointe-à-Pitre and Atlanta.[77] In January 1986, three weeks before he died, he went abroad for the very last time, this time to Yaoundé. A photograph shows him at the end of his presentation being carried in triumph by enthusiastic young Cameroonians who to this day largely subscribe to his world-views.

Between his trips abroad, he staged numerous public events on scientific issues in Senegal: firstly, at a symposium about his work, organized by the editors of the Sankoré series of the publisher Pathé Diagne, secondly during the 'Days of Reflection' about the relationship between religion and philosophy, and also during the Cultural Week at the College for Young Girls in Thiès, where he spoke about *Làmmiñi réew mi ak gëstu*, or 'national languages and scientific research.' In addition to that topic, this lecture also contains a singularly lucid summary in Wolof of many years of reflection in various fields of human knowledge.

Diop died suddenly in Dakar on February 7, 1986. A huge crowd accompanied him to Caytu, his native village and his grave has become a place of pilgrimage for all his followers.

In a certain sense, the month of December 1981 can serve as a point of reference for those who want to convey a few carefully chosen words about the legacy of the two men. It is the date when President Senghor had just resigned and Cheikh Anta Diop had only four years left to live.

As soon as the poet had 'left the limelight', a discreet de-Senghorization started to take place, as we have seen. The political landscape was changing and the sub-prefects in the small villages in the interior gradually lost interest in Leo Frobenius and the lofty organ blasts of Claudel's poetry. In his peaceful retreat in Normandy, Senghor remained silent. He stayed true to his word that he would henceforth stay out of Senegalese politics until the end and his compatriots were grateful to him for his dignified reserve. When you have been the head of government of a country for so long, you need a certain amount of moral grace and character to be able to keep such a promise. And very slowly, with the passage of time, people seem to be changing their minds and seeing him in a more favourable light. Instead of remembering his petty little political shortcomings of so long ago, people salute him for the historic role he played and the fact that he managed to give Senegalese society a direction. After endless accusations that his regime was the most corrupt in the world, it was eventually discovered that he in fact never used his position as head of State to plunder the national Treasury. This fact, quite rare in Africa and elsewhere, deserves to be emphasized. And when on March 29, 1984, he was admitted to the *Académie Française,* the whole of Senegal felt extremely proud of him. Every time he returned to the country in order to participate in some cultural event, his presence, be it at a theatre or anywhere else, attracted large crowds of people and ordinary citizens were clamouring to pay him their respects. The more cultured members of society, especially the visual artists, made a public spectacle of their unhappiness about his departure. And over the years, all of us started to feel this nagging nostalgia for the Senghor era, above all because of what he had done for the promotion of the Arts and the Humanities.

His successor Abdou Diouf, by contrast, is considered as a cold technocrat with little concern for artistic achievements.

To all this, one must add an unmistakable sign and that is that to this very day, the truly unconditional Senghor devotees are those who were most closely associated with him in every-day life. Such loyalty is a precious testimony of Senghor's personal qualities. He is always portrayed as a man who would listen to everything and everybody, who was courteous, methodical and fair. On June 7, 1981, the death in an accident of his son Philippe-Maguilen aroused an immense wave of sympathy among the population and he succeeded in not letting his pain get the better of him.[78] A friend of mine told me about her conversation with Senghor on the day when she went to express her condolences at 'Jaws', his Dakar residence.[79] He simply told her, in a shaky but calm voice, "I have had everything in my life and I can understand that after giving me so much, God wanted to put me to the test by taking away the being who was closest to my heart."

His final years were probably not easy. According to the revelations of a Senegalese intellectual who had the privilege of being in contact with him until the end of his life, Senghor, in his twilight years, almost doubted his place in history. It seems that he was feeling utterly alone and forsaken. Today, it is crystal clear to everyone that there was no reason for his concern. Apart from his own country, a sizeable part of the African continent is paying tribute to him as someone who managed to build a State and knew how to govern his country successfully and with moderation, but not without a firm hand. As a Catholic, he had also succeeded in becoming a symbol of national unity in a Senegal which was overwhelmingly Muslim. If this does not serve as proof of his open-mindedness, nothing will.

Another thing which is easily forgotten is the fact that Senghor was seventeen years older than Cheikh Anta Diop and that he lived thirty three years longer than he did. That is quite some time. In fact, it is only Diop's exceptionally precocious mind which can explain why they are generally seen as thinkers belonging to the same generation or as being more or less the same age. To be able to complete such a colossal amount of work, Diop must have been haunted night and day by his thoughts and ideas and must have worked obsessively, sometimes very close to breaking point. As the initiator of a veritable cultural revolution, he imagined that his enemies were constantly looking over his shoulder, frantically trying to trip him up. Diop was only able to survive so much hatred and suspicion thanks to his unusual strength of spirit. But such Herculean challenges burn up your entire being and don't allow you to live very long.[80] Cheikh Anta Diop knew and accepted this. It may have been the exact opposite for Senghor, whose serenity had amazed

Césaire even in their youth. He was less dangerous to the establishment and probably less keen to force his destiny. Diop wanted to move mountains while Senghor was busy ploughing his own furrow, slowly, but a little deeper every day. While Diop never lost a single minute, his muscles never relaxed and the violent effort made him grimace, Senghor allowed things to take their course. With such incompatible rhythms governing their lives, one might say that they didn't really inhabit the same universe.

A second, major difference makes any comparison between the two very difficult. We have all seen Senghor at work as Senegal's head of State and it is up to us what we think of it. As far as Cheikh Anta Diop is concerned, no one can tell what sort of president of the Republic he would have been. Having good ideas is one thing, but governing a country is quite another. Being a statesman requires certain qualities – and perhaps more importantly, certain flaws! –that can only be judged on actual evidence. Diop was often praised for the clarity of his intentions. This must have been an advantage over Senghor, who was sometimes forced against his will to take unpopular decisions. On the other hand, actually being in power would definitely have been a lot more difficult for Diop. In those days, a progressive Developing World leader used to spend more energy fighting the western intelligence services than on implementing his programme.

Senghor never had any such worries, because he was on the right side. He often prided himself on having won our independence "after a one-hour talk with General de Gaulle." Is that just a simple way of telling the tale? One would love to believe it. But let's not forget that Senghor was also an ingenious artist – perhaps he was being serious. He may have believed his own fairy tale about having negotiated our liberation in the gilded halls of the Elysée Palace. But one just doesn't end three centuries of brutal colonial occupation with a brief exchange of pleasantries. During those Cold War years, a serious pledge of good conduct was required, particularly if you wanted to be in charge of Senegal, which in some way for France was the jewel in its crown. This leaves us with the open question whether Senghor, who had patience and who was more inclined to subterfuge than confrontation, was planning a gradual infiltration of the colonial system which he wanted to expand over time. If this was his secret plan, he was not given the opportunity – as was perfectly predictable – to put it into practice. But in reality, we must doubt this. This idea of blowing up the enemy fortress from within is the sort of thing the hagiographers like to suggest retrospectively to make their story less depressing. Unfortunately, when it comes to his relationship with France, it is extremely hard to be kind to Senghor. It is simply a fact that this man, who was in charge of our country for twenty years, openly boasted about having the nationality of the ex-colonizer. Why then and wherefore? Purely in order to be admitted to the Académie Française… Whatever angle we take to look at this decision, it is not acceptable. And it is even less acceptable, considering the fact that the reputation of the Académie Française is largely overrated. But even if it had been the most dynamic centre of knowledge and reflection on planet earth, it would have made no difference; as a former head of a State, you remain a symbol. One simply does not, towards the end of one's life, throw to the wind everything one stood for, in order to put on a green suit and live the cosy life of an elderly dignitary in Normandy.[81] It seems that Cheikh Anta Diop never made any official comments on this sad story. But one can well imagine that it would have elicited an acerbic little smile from him. In his eyes, Senghor's nationality was an ethical issue and he mentioned it at every opportunity. For example when, during his battle against the RND, Senghor wanted to deprive the members of 'subversive associations' of their civic rights, Diop told him dryly that a president who could be at the same time Senegalese and French was not morally qualified to talk about civic rights and responsibilities.

Everybody in Senegal is extremely familiar with the names of these two men. But Senghor, who, on his home ground, was more in the public eye due to his presidential position, was also very widely known as a thinker of the 20th century. It is therefore possible that the Senegalese people know him better than Cheikh Anta Diop. Diop was an accomplished thinker who helped to make sense of the hopes and the fury of a huge number of Blacks all over the world. His influence soon started to move very far beyond the francophone territory. But this does not change the fact that Diop is a slightly disembodied figure. About the man himself, we know very little, even in his own country. The books that have been written about him usually focus on his mind. This state of affairs, which is largely due to his profound humility, is nevertheless a problem. It is regrettable for a number of reasons. The president of the Dia Council, for example, made a speech after his death, where he presented him as a role model for young Africans. But how, one wonders, can they use him as their inspiration if they know nothing about his ordinary daily life, his doubts and his weaknesses? Like every one of us, Cheikh Anta Diop was the product of a specific set of familial, social and political circumstances. The secret of his personal greatness lies in the unique alchemy of adhesion to and resistance against these structural elements. This is why it is so important to understand, in as much detail as possible, how his rejection of false evidence turned him into a revolutionary in the purest sense of the word and precisely how, very gradually, the Promethean ambition was born in him to completely change our worldview.

Moreover, one sometimes has the impression that his work stirs up a stronger reaction outside Senegal than among his own people. In Dakar, just one day has been set aside to celebrate the anniversary of his death, whereas the young people of Burkina Faso are spending the whole month of February celebrating the occasion with lectures and other cultural events. The Mayor of Atlanta has dedicated a day in his honour and in many central African countries one can find groups which discuss and think about the legacy of Cheikh Anta Diop. If there are similar groups in Senegal, they can neither be very numerous nor very dynamic.

What is the reason for this imbalance? Perhaps it is due to a possible misunderstanding between the Egyptologist and the Senegalese Marxists, who accused both him and Senghor of the same flaw, even though politically, they were a lot closer to Diop. They did not like their predominantly cultural approach. At the symposium organized by the publisher Sankoré in 1982, he was hard pressed during the debate to convince many of them, especially the philosophers, to drop their reservations,.. But be that as it may, the liveliness of the debate itself was proof of the fact that a new generation of academics had acknowledged his work and had a critical opinion about it.

He is also often criticized for his stubbornness regarding Ancient Egypt, while Africa today is such a calamity. These are unfair allegations against a man who always made a point of not separating the past from the future, who was constantly making sure he was dealing with facts rather than emotions and talking about what had actually happened as opposed to what ought to have happened. No one understood better than he did the need to confront, right here and now, the many problems assailing the continent. Clearly, it is extremely unfair to reduce Cheikh Anta Diop's legacy to the theory about the precedence of the Black civilizations. It may be true that his research in this area forms the basis on which his perception of our destiny is built, but his contributions to a variety of fields go far beyond the narrow confines of this single topic. The Pan Africanist dream for example, was popularized by Kwame Nkrumah, Julius Nyerere, Amilcar Cabral, Sékou Touré and other progressive leaders. But Diop is the person who gave this idea a solid scientific foundation. One of his books, to which he himself refers quite frequently, explicitly deals with this issue.

The cultural unity of Africa South of the Sahara is one important argument in favour of Cheikh Anta Diop's proposition to create an African federation. As he was able to demonstrate, it is based on the close relationship between ancient Egyptian and African languages. Among the great thinkers and politicians of his time, Diop was the only one to have recognized the linguistic question as being of primary importance. He saw the national languages as playing a crucial role in the unification as well as the liberation of the African peoples and considered the fact that they had been largely abandoned by the elites as an irrefutable sign of alienation.

Everybody today and especially former South African president Thabo Mbeki, talks about the 'African Renaissance' as though it was a complete novelty and an ideal to aspire to. Cheikh Anta Diop not only started developing this concept in 1948, but he also explained that for it to become reality we have to restore our sense of history and re-establish a certain historical continuity.[82]

He has sometimes been portrayed as a gentle utopian or even an unusual dreamer who always said very wise things! One example being that no African country should pretend to be able to resolve its economic and political problems by itself. He was much more pragmatic than most people imagine and he summed up his point of view about this in the famous sentence: 'Even an enlightened form of egoism militates for a Federal State of Africa.'

This means that we are missing the point when we talk about 'Egyptolatry' in connection with him – someone came across this word somewhere. Let's just pretend for a moment that Cheikh Anta Diop has never written a single word about Ancient Egypt. In the light of what has already been mentioned – his proposed federation, the importance of the national languages, etc. – his contribution to the thinking about Africa would have been no less significant. There are some critical commentaries that are not particularly constructive. They will definitely not ensure that Diop's work, which is increasingly falling victim to its own phenomenal success, is given a kinder reception. The fact that black Africans play such a central historical role in it, makes it particularly appealing for certain militant extremists who are fighting for the Black cause. It is not surprising that Cheikh Anta Diop experts are not happy about this. They remind us at every opportunity that he never described himself as an Afrocentrist and did not even like the word, nor would he, according to them, ever have been so bold as to suggest Blacks were superior in any shape or form. He equally never intended to take revenge by proxy for the pain and the humiliations of the past. That is to say that in his view, we are more likely to regain our sense of history through the determination to tame the future than by self-pity and harking back to the past. This reading of Diop's work shows its objectivity cannot be doubted. He basically says the same things in his written texts, during interviews and in his recorded lectures. It was always his opinion that any human community living in similar conditions to those of the Blacks of Egypt would have behaved the same way, adding, for the sake of clarity: "Insofar as we can talk about race." On the other hand, putting the mirror back in place did not mean for Diop that Blacks should see themselves as more beautiful than the rest.

The question remains whether this guardedly ecumenical point of view is shared by the majority in the vast movement which was sparked by the ideas of the author of *Black Nations and Culture.* One does not have the impression that it is, nor is it apparent how it could be otherwise. Against a background of mounting negrophobia and revisionism, Diop's thinking has obviously had a polarizing effect on every continent where the black Diaspora has a presence. This in turn has fuelled a black neo-radicalism, which can be very vehement at times. From various different directions, loud, aggressive voices are calling this the best antidote against the kind of humanism that has been perceived as a new eurocentric hoax. Not only does this intellectual movement form an integral part of Cheikh Anta Diop's heritage, but it is also a testimony to the vigour and freshness of his ideas, which is why it undoubtedly deserves universal expansion. In all likelihood, this would have been Diop's wish. Sadly we find that such a noble ambition would stand a better chance of becoming reality in a world quite unlike ours. Never in history and nowhere among all the nations of this planet has human life been as far removed from the ideal of 'the good man' as now. With or without globalization, we simply do not know where the madness of mankind will lead us. And, whether we care to admit it or not, everybody is just running for cover, because a storm is brewing. So people are running for shelter until the sky has cleared, although they don't know if or when that will happen. In essence, the run-of-the-mill politics of today can be described as increasingly ferocious confrontations about identity. To allow such a blindingly obvious problem to escalate is clearly very unwise. And although the worries about the possibility of an obstinate racial isolation are understandable, the other alternative, which would be a sort of gradual "Senghorization" of Cheikh Anta Diop's philosophy, is just as undesirable. If that were to happen, it would be terribly ironic. For those black Africans who are feeling offended and humiliated, cultural resistance is more imperative than ever, and the new perspectives that have opened up thanks to Diop will ensure their battle is effective. The debate about our past, which he initiated, is closely linked with the image we have of ourselves at the moment. For better or for worse, the richness and complexity of his world view continues to attract a great variety of people.

Interpretations of Diop's work are frequently so far-fetched or grossly exaggerated that safeguards against this kind of thing would be very welcome. Certain people who are hardly qualified to do so are now meddling with the evaluation of Cheikh Anta Diop's legacy and even, it seems, proclaiming its infallibility. This gives Diop's adversaries an excellent pretext to exclude him from scientific research altogether. We cannot allow just anybody to come along and decide about hugely complex questions that require cross-referencing in various different disciplines. Any sort of apotheosis runs counter to the methodology of a scientist who must be very well aware that he has to back up his theories with hard evidence if he does not want to risk his credibility. I am personally perfectly happy to confess that I lack the competence that would be required to judge this particular aspect of Cheikh Anta Diop's work. However, even a lay person can say this, which is simply common sense: if new discoveries come to light – archaeological ones, for example – the balance could tip in his opponents' favour at any moment. The man in question never tried to contradict this. If Cheikh Anta Diop had been afraid that the facts might prove him wrong, he would never have instigated the Cairo symposium in 1974. By inviting their western colleagues to a presentation of their mutual findings, Diop and Obenga accomplished a feat of exceptional symbolic significance. Perhaps it has never been emphasized enough, but it was a way of freeing us from all the superficial ideological claptrap which allows people to hide behind their own convictions, looking for gullible supporters who are willing to agree with their conclusions before the demonstration has even begun. It has been mentioned before, but it is important to say again that this perilous encounter on the banks of the Nile undeniably ended with a clear victory for Diop and Obenga. Professor Jean Devisse's report clearly states that "The content of the preliminary paper submitted by UNESCO did not change the fact that the exceptionally detailed presentation by professors Cheikh Anta Diop and Théophile Obenga was in a class of its own. This caused a distinct imbalance during the discussions." Not only in Africa, but also among black populations elsewhere, could those who are still doubtful – either due to a sense of intellectual superiority or – inferiority – please stand up and say what more they could possibly want? What further scientific venture would they like us to tackle?

The Cairo encounter took place thirty-two years ago and since then, nothing has weakened Cheikh Anta Diop's main premise in any way. Quite on the contrary. Despite all sorts of derisory ploys, many new discoveries have in fact reinforced its validity. One of those was made public in the prestigious science journal *Nature* on February 6, 1986, literally twenty-four hours before Cheikh Anta Diop's death… by a team of British scientists. Ivan Van Sertima, author of the famous book *They Came Before Columbus*, mentions it in a moving, perfectly worded homage. Here is what he writes in the introduction of a book entirely devoted to Cheikh Anta Diop:[83] 'We quote now from a document published on the day before Diop's death. It is entitled *Evolutionary Relationships of Human Populations from an Analysis of* Nuclear *DNA Polymorphisms.* It is the work of eleven scientists, most of them from the University of Oxford, England and it appears in *Nature*, vol. 319 (February 6, 1986). The team of scientists concluded, "The earliest fossils of anatomically modern man (Homo sapiens sapiens) have been found in Africa at Omo in Ethiopia, Border cave in South Africa and at Klasies River Mouth in South Africa. […]. Hence, it has been argued that the evolution of modern man took place in Africa. Our data is consistent with such a scheme, in which a founder population migrated from Africa and subsequently gave rise to all non-African populations."'

In the mid-1980s, *Caaxaan Faaxe,* one of Senghor's party political journals, had the audacity to nickname Cheikh Anta Diop 'the madman of Fann', thereby alluding to the proximity between his laboratory and the biggest psychiatric hospital of Dakar. The crudeness of this insult could not conceal the attempt to persuade the public that he was a loner living in cloud-cuckoo-land who had lost his grip on reality. This view is very widespread, particularly in Senegal, albeit in a rather more polite form. And equally frequently, Diop is described as a man of pure knowledge who was all the less cut out for politics since his sense of morals was slightly too highly developed. If he had heard this kind of thing, there is no doubt that he would have locked himself up in his laboratory for the rest of his life. Luckily, his great insight helped him avoid such a fatal mistake. As a matter of fact, he was forced very early to perceive his twin intellectual and political engagement as one entity. Since his opponents used mostly political arguments against him, he felt obliged to fight them on the same ground, but he never stopped pursuing his research with all the necessary diligence.

The media ruled the roost in those days and Senghor was constantly in the news and celebrated, whether it was in the governmental daily, on television, or the radio. Cheikh Anta Diop, like the rest of the political opposition, was *persona non grata.*[84] Barred from any possibility of transmitting his knowledge, he would have been even more isolated had he stayed away from the political platform. Considering all these attempts to marginalize him, it is remarkable that Diop managed to make himself heard to such an extent.

All of Cheikh Anta Diop's old comrades attest that he was not a power hungry man. And he was probably aware that only a very exceptional chain of events could have propelled him to the top position of the Senegalese State. In the fight against his most obstinate opponents, Senghor was able to rely on Paris, the true mastermind, for support. Diop, however, paved the way for the future, turning political activism into a medium for education and the dissemination of his ideas. Here we have an approach which is diametrically opposed to that of the 'brainless elites' Césaire talks about and who are holding African populations hostage.[85] He felt that Africa needed a new breed of leaders who would assist the continent in recovering its freedom, prosperity and pride. He knew how to preach by example and one can say that his message was well received by his compatriots. To the ordinary Senegalese citizen, Diop managed to convey a very pleasing picture of himself as a politician. Altruistic and sure of himself, without being arrogant, he never yielded to the temptation of using invective and bullying tactics. In retrospect, he gives the impression of having been a peace-loving iconoclast, a warrior always in the centre of the fray, but equally at home in his study, leading the solitary life of the scholar. Twenty years after his death, we are left with the memory of a man who lived under relentless, self-imposed moral tension, light-years away from the worldly temptations of money and fame.

More out of youthful curiosity than anything else, many of us in my generation initially just saw him as a benevolent, open-minded Elder and it was only much later that we began to grasp the profound originality of his political battle. Although I had – briefly and on a modest scale – been an activist in the National Democratic Union, I was predominantly keen to hear him speak at every opportunity. It was extremely easy to gain access to him, at the Carbon-14 laboratory. From midday onwards, the door of his study stayed symbolically open and everybody and anybody could go and see him. One could just take a seat on one of the benches in the corridor and wait one's turn, without any need to make an appointment. Many of his visitors were simple people from the rural areas. Cheikh Anta Diop didn't intimidate these peasants, who were either members of his party, or distant relatives. His uncommon intelligence was obvious from his penetrating gaze, but he also had a great deal of empathy and never took advantage of this. He always listened very attentively to what his visitors had to say. While often showing signs of fatigue, his face never, as far as I remember, betrayed even the slightest hint of impatience at the exasperating ignorance he had to contend with. But in the end, he was struck down by a heart attack, a day after one of these encounters.

One would sometimes like to indulge in a little reverie about a reconciliation between Cheikh Anta Diop and Senghor in the hereafter. This idea of a posthumous ceasefire, conceived by some of his heirs, is noble enough and it even makes a certain amount of sense. Both of these two ambassadors of culture served the black African world in their own particular way, using the means at their disposal. And it is clear that many of their compatriots have an equal admiration for them.

But hanging on to this notion also means losing sight of some other, similarly crucial aspects of their conflict. The fact that two such radically different personalities of this calibre should have emerged from the depths of the same nation says a lot about the ambiguity of the latter. This, too, is a problem and we have to be courageous enough to confront it. To try to reconcile the opinions of Diop and Senghor at all costs comes down to a refusal to accept the contradictions and the paradoxes, as well as the essential perversity of Senegalese society. To play off one against the other is not the point here, but rather to show respect for the life and vision of each of them in his own right. At the same time, it would be silly to pretend that there have never been profound differences of opinion between the two of them. For now, it will suffice if everybody clearly states his preference for one of the two men and his respective point of view. The verdict of future generations will no doubt be more reliable than that of the present one. As the philosopher so neatly said, "the future lasts a long time."[86] As humans, we like to listen to the whispers of destiny, although they are hard to decipher and almost inaudible. But that's no reason to stop trying. In conclusion, one could perhaps say that if Senghor has admirers, Cheikh Anta Diop has disciples. Senghor, the immortal master of the French language and true leader of men, largely deserves the veneration his name evokes, despite the fact that his dark side threw long shadows. And Diop's acolytes, for their part, are working hard on the tangible results of his research, which are opening up the way to so many exciting new ventures while at the same time allowing us to feel that the steps we take are on much firmer ground. And now it is basically our task to continue with his work, which is the best way of proving wrong the friend who wrote to me on a profoundly sad day in February 1986: "With Cheikh Anta Diop's death, for the first time, we have not only lost someone, but also something..."

The New Wretched of the Earth

On February 21, 2005, the *New York Times* carried the headline: "More Africans are entering the United States now than in the days of slavery." If nothing else, the sense of relief in these words is ambiguous, while the comparison is as preposterous as it is dangerous. It is born out of the typically Western sentiment that one is tired of playing the Good Samaritan for the poor from all over the world and wondering when this is at last going to end.

This attitude also explains the brutality of the Spanish police in dealing with the stowaway migrants at Ceuta and Melilla in September and October 2005. One remembers television crews from all over the world, virtually salivating as they were filming thick, blood-stained gloves entangled in barbed wire, young Africans stumbling around in the desert lost and dazed and – just to complete the picture – some charitable souls offering them pastries behind the iron bars of makeshift reception centres.

Events before the cameras arrived had been even more dramatic. In successive waves, several thousands of migrants from Africa South of the Sahara had tried to storm the sophisticated border protection. Roughly 200 of them had managed to get into Spain near Tarajal on September 28, at a cost of 5 deaths and dozens wounded.

In Melilla, too, attempts at entering by force had multiplied. Out of nearly 1500 migrants – mostly from Mali, but also from Cameroon, Ivory Coast and Liberia – between 300 and 400 had slipped through the net of the Guardia Civil. On September 29, at 3:30 a.m., a skilful manoeuvre by their comrades gave roughly 700 of the Ceuta migrants the chance to try their luck with shaky ladders: 6 of them lost their lives.

There is nothing exceptional about clashes such as this one. From the beginning of 2005 onwards, nearly 20,000 young people from the Maghreb or Africa South of the Sahara were making regular attempts to cross into Europe on learning that the height of the wire-netting would be increased from 3.5 to 6 metres.

The number of casualties – 16 fatalities and hundreds of wounded according to official sources – was less shocking than the scandalous decision to lead the migrants into the desert with the obvious intention of letting them die there. The image of young black Africans chained to one another is bound to bring back some bad memories on the continent. The only difference is that now, instead of forcibly shipping them to the West, one forcibly tries to keep them out of the West.

The resulting outcry eventually forced Morocco to soften its stance, but the damage had been done. Ten days after these incidents, rather than being treated humanely, the illegals were still being tossed back and forth like so much garbage. More bodies were recovered, like those of two Guineans who had died from exhaustion, on October 17. They had been part of several groups – including one of 398 people on October 20 – that were being pushed back to Morocco by the Algerians, who were of course delighted to make things difficult for their neighbour and arch enemy.

If the main perpetrator of this crime was Morocco, aided and abetted by Algeria, then Spain and the European Union acted as their tacit collaborators. It makes one wonder when countries that claim to be constantly on the look-out for Human Rights infringements in every corner of the globe fail so dismally in their duty to protect human lives.

The countries of the North have two great fears – terrorism and immigration – and it seems as though the wish to keep the Europeans calm is increasingly overriding the importance of everything else. It would clearly be naive to mention ethics, but in dealing with a modern State, one ought to be able to expect a modicum of rationality.

Right now, the politicians of the Old Continent are obsessed with just one issue and that is the elections in their respective countries: above all, one has to create the impression that something is being done, even if it means just making empty gestures. In the peculiar way he moves his chin and furrows his brow while uttering sweeping statements, Nicolas Sarkozy, the French Minister of the Interior, is trying to come across as a strong and fearless leader – the only one in his country bold enough to cut the Gordian Knot. And yet, he is veering towards exactly the same impasse as his predecessors, the only difference being that he has more bounce in his step, but his puffed up chest makes him look quite ridiculous. One really must hope that sooner or later a "sane" French politician will manage to give the National Front immigration programme some credibility. If his taste for offensive, hurtful and obscene remarks was the only thing Nicolas Sarkozy had in common with M. Le Pen, nobody would mind. But unfortunately, his law which has just been passed by the French Parliament has to be taken seriously. Besides other reforms, it stipulates that immigrants have both their language skills and their intellectual abilities tested before France can "choose" to clasp them to her bosom. It is hard not to be reminded of the time when young Blacks were put up for sale in the slave markets, patted, weighed and also "chosen," solely for the purpose of fulfilling the white master's requirements. By encouraging African doctors and engineers to leave their continent for France's benefit we are only aggravating the problem we are pretending to resolve. This way of thinking is as perverse as it is brutal. It means African societies can starve to death while M. Sarkozy is looking the other way.

But this particular part of the law has probably been publicized in advance for a reason. By focusing on this section, one easily forgets all the other measures destined to make it more difficult to enter and reside in France – all inspired by the assumed culpability of the immigrant. The legislation is based on prejudice: the immigrant is seen as a parasite, steeped in an innate culture of fraud, who has to be prevented from paying for his endless wives and children with money taken out of the pockets of French citizens who, for their part, never stop toiling to make an honest living in the sweat of their brow. Now, it will no longer just be a question of legitimizing those who have no papers and trying to reunite families will become a bureaucratic nightmare. It will also be much harder for foreign students to gain admission to French universities. In April 2006, an article in the *Le Figaro* effectively stated that "bogus students have infiltrated the system, encouraged by the laxity of certain universities which have been abandoned by local students."

This authoritarian bidding for votes was made possible – and politically relevant – by the xenophobia that has been festering in European societies for some years now. Verbal attacks have escalated into police brutalities and then apartment blocks in Paris started to go up in flames. The media no longer get excited by the racist murders of Blacks and Arabs in Paris, Lyon, Anvers or Moscow. In Spain, at its maritime and terrestrial borders with Morocco, many of the 6,500 victims registered on the official casualty lists over the last 10 years were simply slaughtered or secretly thrown to the sharks.

And yet, even this murderous hatred is not enough of a deterrent; each time a point of entry has come to the attention of the authorities, the stowaway migrants manage to find another one. That is why for some months now, they have been using the coastlines of Senegal and Mauritania as points of departure, with the Canary Islands as their destination. At least 5,000 of them were intercepted between January and May 2006. Not a single week goes by anymore without dozens of bodies being washed up on the shore. In the same way, Ceuta and Melilla serve as passageways when the Straits of Gibraltar and the coast of Italy are deemed too dangerous. Between June 2003 and September 2005, close to 600 migrants died there by drowning and this number does not include bodies which were never recovered. And then there is the issue of boats that the coast guards sink deliberately in this area as well as at all the other maritime points of entry such as Greece, Malta or Cyprus.

Joe Soap, who is regularly exposed to these television images, inevitably starts to fear that Europe's peace and prosperity is being invaded by successive waves of starving young black Africans. He does not seem to be aware that *all* the impoverished African and Asian nations are represented among the *boat people* on the Sicilian coast. Until recently, North Africans outnumbered everybody else in Ceuta and Melilla

This last statement is quite explosive considering the fact that Algeria, Morocco, Libya and Mauritania have been accused of sheltering migrants from parts of Africa South of the Sahara that are very far removed from Europe. Colonel Muammar Gaddafi has exploited this situation by procuring a certificate of good conduct towards Europe for himself. Morocco is negotiating a hefty price for its participation in this hunt. The country has received 40 million euros for playing a role that should be repugnant to its national pride.[87] But this has not earned Morocco the trust of Madrid, which suspects the puny little kingdom of having secretly instigated the migrants of Ceuta and Melilla to take action in October 2005. At the time, the Spanish daily *El Mundo* echoed these concerns in Spain as follows: "The most worrying aspect is undoubtedly the fact that this series of assaults seems to be part of a strategy by the Moroccans to put pressure on the Spanish-Moroccan summit which is about to start at Cordoba."

The outsourcing of anti-emigrant violence to North Africa, superimposed on the massacres targeted at Darfur is likely to leave enormous psychological damage in its wake in the long run. These images of Blacks being pursued by Arabs are too high a price to pay simply to preserve Europe's peace of mind.

It is particularly unacceptable since nothing at the time justified the fear of a massive onslaught of stowaways on Europe via the Sahara or the Mediterranean. That was a pure figment of the imagination; for the two previous years, numbers at the International Migration Office were clearly indicating a downward trend.

Madrid counted 12,000 attempts at illegal border crossings in 2005 versus 55,000 in 2004. The same thing was happening along the Italian coast: 3,000 arrivals were registered in 2004 versus 6,350 in 2002. But we know that since May 2006, all these numbers have become obsolete. As a matter of fact, a complete reversal of the situation has occurred. The invasion of Europe, just a trickle at the beginning of the year, has sharply accelerated: every day, hundreds of young migrants from Africa South of the Sahara, arrive in Spain on their rickety boats after embarking on the shores of Senegal, Mauritania or Gambia. It is a fairly dangerous undertaking, but the vast majority made it to their destination. In mid-June, the Spanish authorities stated that there had been 10,156 new arrivals on their territory. This tide, which at present nothing seems to be able to stem, has condemned Ceuta and Melilla to oblivion virtually over night. It continues to throw the Spanish government into the most profound disarray and has even caused verbal hostilities between Madrid and Paris.[88]

Clearly, this new state of affairs obliges us to rethink everything, but one must not lose sight of the fact that according to the experts, the majority of immigrants from any country are entering Europe legally. The French Minister of the Interior has set himself the goal of 24,000 expulsions per year. But he has to take into account that during that same period, at least an identical number of migrants without papers will be swelling the ranks of those already in France – and their number has been estimated at between 200,000 and 400,000…

In France itself, the Sarkozy Law has aroused strong reactions. The Church and more than 400 organizations have taken a stand against it on ethical grounds and from the point of view of human rights and mere hospitality. But according to the opinion polls the majority of the French people are in favour of it. Solely the concept of 'immigration by choice' seems to pose a problem for the rest, for very odd reasons: some reproach the minister for his generosity while professionals say they fear the competition of highly trained foreigners prepared to accept very low salaries in their fields of expertise.

One is of course dumbfounded by these nasty tactics…

The new law, by the way, was introduced as a partial answer to the revolt in the suburbs.

Even its wording shows that it is really all about the question of integration. What it also shows is that it is becoming difficult to legislate on this issue today, trying to disguise a colonial past which is still weighing down an entire nation. This refusal to accept a painful history with a degree of equanimity is hard to understand. Those who want to camouflage the Slave Trade and the colonial heritage of France are threatening to turn every debate about immigration and the revolt in the suburbs into a farce.

It makes sense that the word "memory" does not have the same connotations for everybody in a country with such a recent history of expansionism. It is because of that very past that in Aubervilliers or in Montreuil one can be *legally* French, while having to ask oneself constantly whether one has the right skin colour.

Nevertheless, the Blacks who 'smell [bad]' according to journalist Marc-Olivier Fogiel,[89] just like the 'sub-humans' of the socialist Member of Parliament Georges Frêche, have no native country other than France. The clauses of the Sarkozy Law do not concern them in any way, except for the word 'foreigner' which figures in it and is addressed far more directly to them than to some of their other compatriots. It is they who were shocked, sometimes without ever having set foot on the Antilles, in Algiers or Abidjan, by the law about the 'positive aspects of colonialization' and by the scandalously denialist books about the Slave Trade. It is they who prick up their ears when they hear the word *Françafrique*. They understand why their ancestors came to France a long time ago and why they themselves feel as though they are caught in an infernal trap there. Nor does one have to explain to them that the looting of the resources of the countries of emigration by the French State did not stop with the advent of those who came to power at independence, quite on the contrary. This frequently meant that governments, not necessarily all of them as the example of Senegal demonstrates, required economic support. As a result, the hopes and expectations of the youth were undermined and their development stunted. Without that, many would not have chosen to go into exile.

On a much larger scale, the global economic system has exacerbated the North-South disparities. The destruction of agriculture and the civil service went hand in hand with the privatization of businesses and public services for the benefit of the multinationals that had sprung up on the continent.

The large number of Malians among the migrants should come as no surprise. Although their country is one of the three top cotton-producing countries in Africa, it is nevertheless also one of the poorest places on the planet. In 2005, these peasants were selling their cotton at a price of 160 francs CFA per kg compared to 210 francs CFA the year before. By prohibiting the African producer countries from subsidizing this industry while giving their own farmers financial support, the rich countries have a lot to answer for about this state of affairs.

The case of the cotton industry is just one of many examples which are so typical of the South-North imbalances. Every time the G8 countries get together, the 'total' cancellation of Africa's debt is announced. And then they usually promise to increase the development aid budget and on top of that – no laughing! – additional programmes for the protection of human rights.

These different approaches to the same problem have one thing in common: Africans are never allowed to solve their own problems. Instead of forcing them into the role of eternal recipients of assistance, certain European countries should rather give up their private hunting grounds in Africa by ceasing to prop up and arm the rogue states with which they share – so illegitimately – the continent's natural resources.

The African heads of government, having been made both accomplices and beneficiaries of this iniquitous system, do not dare to complain about the ill treatment inflicted on their subjects at the gateway to the Schengen countries. At any rate, Europe knows that she can do what she likes in Africa without being held accountable by those puppets that a French comedian recently referred to as 'negro kings'.

African civil society itself is frequently mute when faced with the massacres of young Somalians, Liberians and Moroccans along the European coastline. Having said that, on October 14, 2005 in Bamako, Aminata Traoré, leader of the Alterglobalization Movement in Africa, set off on a 'March for Dignity' which took her to Brussels via Paris, Milan and Madrid. In all these capital cities, she and her Malian companions protested against the increasingly criminal control of the floods of migrants. But such initiatives are relatively rare. One feels that on the European continent, the outcasts of Ceuta and Melilla are equally excluded from the battle for human rights. Behind the racial smoke screen, it is easy to see the purely political dimension of this problem. The migrants are not just African Blacks, they are in equal measure simply destitute. Where they come from, the political and intellectual elites don't want to hear about their plight. At times, these new wretched of the earth have the feeling that there is even less room for them in their own, totally bankrupt societies, than elsewhere.

Nevertheless, it seems as though a change is imminent. Every member of a group of 21 activists from the Malian political elite publicly declared his or her opposition to Nicolas Sarkozy's visit to Bamako on May 17, 2006. This allowed the public to understand more clearly that the foreign policy of France in Africa is at the heart of the debate about immigration. One hopes that once he has stirred up violent protest action from Fort-de-France to Bamako and probably elsewhere in the former Empire, Sarkozy will begin to see the extraordinary complexity of problems which he thinks he can resolve in an instant.

It is generally assumed that the migrants are trying to escape from ethnic conflicts and dictatorial regimes. That, however, is by no means always the case. Senegal and Mali, both of which provide large contingents of candidates for this journey, are two relatively peaceful and democratic countries. The truth is that the vast majority of migrants have been driven away from their homes because of poverty. The 'Promised Land' that they see every night on television makes them realize the deprivations of their daily lives. That is how they conceive the desire to seek out distant horizons, encouraged by those who, having got *over there*, pretend that everything is marvellous. Northerners seem to find it hard to fathom the sheer power of this aspiration to a better life. They prefer to think that, if certain countries are poor, it is their own fault. Looking back over the centuries, is it not a little bit simplistic to pretend that the West owes its wealth exclusively to its own hard labour? Today, for mysterious reasons, Europeans are prepared to listen to just about anything except the fact that they are largely responsible for the economic disasters that have created the chaos at their borders.

Having said this, one also has to ask oneself why these young people, some of whom have some educational qualifications, seem to be prepared to pay with their lives for the hypothetical prospect of gaining access to the Schengen space, even if it means being stoned and clubbed by vast numbers of heavily armed Moroccan and Spanish soldiers. Having to watch, over and over again, the spectacle of these pitiful souls in exile who are treated like animals and barely know whether they are alive or dead, is utterly intolerable. One cannot but feel shame and anguish, combined with a helpless rage, looking at these clandestines. It is difficult to understand why a young African, ready to die so he can leave home, is never prepared to suffer in order to improve the place he comes from to the benefit of future generations.

But it would probably be wrong to explain this suicidal behaviour exclusively with the attraction of Europe. It seems more likely that these migrants have fallen into a trap from which they cannot escape. Invariably, before they have even arrived on the Canaries or at the barbed wire fences of Ceuta and Melilla, the passengers have handed over every penny they had to shady ferrymen and border-guards. The price is in the region of one thousand euros and according to an Italian legal expert, the revenue from this trafficking via Sicily alone has been estimated to amount to around ten million dollars per year. And one must not forget the long and difficult trips across the desert, either on foot or on clapped-out, overcrowded lorries. After that comes the hardest part: the anxious wait and precarious survival in the forests of Gourougou and Bel Younes. There, they become part of a community and friendships develop around their dreams of Europe, so close and yet so far. The certainty that the Eldorado will come, either now or never, grows stronger by the day. Is there a human being who, crushed by poverty, can possibly resist the illusion that by braving some barbed wire he can change his own life and the lives of his loved-ones at home forever? Before passing judgment on these migrants from the comfort and ease of a normal life, this is the question one has to ask oneself. They don't want to be seen as wimps by their companions, but they also know that the system will never allow them to return to the little shack they left behind. After what happened in Ceuta and Melilla, it is amazing to hear many of them saying: "I had no idea that it was going to be like this, it was unbearable, but every time I wanted to turn back, the others advised me to go on." It's dreadful to have to say this, but no matter what the difficulties are, the migrant is condemned to go forward. Of course it happens that in spite of the suffering and the human losses, there are some who manage to emerge on the other side. This tiny chance of success transforms the way these young people relate to the future into an utterly distressing gamble.

To be aware of this psychological dimension enables us to approach this extremely serious issue in a less emotional way. Thinking about it calmly, you are forced to recognize that Europe seems to have adopted a closed-door policy that in this day and age is simply absurd. As a result, plans are afoot to establish 'immigration portals' or 'support centres' in North Africa: so many euphemisms in order to avoid using the word 'camps', which admittedly carries too much historical baggage. The European Union calls this 'externalizing' the problem of emigration. All these linguistic niceties have failed to completely disguise an oddly belligerent attitude. Europe perceives herself more and more as a beleaguered fortress and will, if necessary, go to extremes to defend herself. Spain is in the process of increasing the size of the barriers protecting its borders again and an enormous moat is going to complete this attempt to make the country secure. This tendency to fall back on one's own resources is perhaps the lesson that has been learnt from repeated rejections by the European Parliament in the course of numerous referendums. Why should one budge to make room for a carpenter from Algeria or Burkina Faso in places where the famous 'Polish plumber' is not welcome?

But be that as it may, administrative measures like this will only make the whole journey more perilous for the clandestine migrants and their numbers are growing daily. They will not stop those who are prepared to brave a thousand dangers in order to get to Europe. What they will do, is swell the bank accounts of the mafia-type gangs of ferrymen without ever getting to the bottom of this major political problem. The issue of emigration is a hard nut to crack and deserves a strategic approach, not a short-term solution dictated by the primordial fear of the *Other* and a certain kind of populism.

In the United States we have seen how an impressive mobilization by the Mexican community has forced president George W. Bush to see some reason. After being initially tempted to lock all the doors, he has now agreed to legitimize eleven million illegal immigrants. On the same occasion, he also announced the deployment of six thousand soldiers at the border. At the end of September, the US Congress was understandably desperate and authorized the erection of a 1,200km wall along the Mexican border. It looks as though the Americans are at a loss how to protect themselves against the poverty of these migrants who have made such a large contribution towards their own prosperity.

That is something little Europe should mull over.

Those who have the arrogance of forcing tens of millions of young people to vegetate in countries that are under pressure themselves are making the world even less secure than it used to be. The forward flight and the egocentricity of the European countries could at some point spawn new forms of violence which, in one way or another, will be to their own detriment. Did we not see unemployed Senegalese men from Rufisque or Thiaroye mounting an assault on the Canary Isles in May 2006, saying they were joining the *Jihad*? For the moment, sadly, that means above all that they will not be able to escape death for long. But such words never become part of the vocabulary of a generation by chance.

A Letter to a Friend about the Sinking of the Joola

Dakar, December 15, 2002

My dear Diadié,

For several weeks now, messages of condolence have been flooding in from everywhere. Some from very close by like yours from Bamako and others from Trinidad or Athens. Through this letter to you, I would like to respond to other friends like Yann and Beata, Louis, Gaoussou and Zohra over there in Vienna, all at the same time.

You have indeed found appropriate and moving words about the tragedy of September 26. I am wondering, though, how much of it a foreigner would remember, one month later. Nowadays it is normal to be bombarded with news about people we have never met, who are trapped under the ruins of some earthquake somewhere very far away. It doesn't even stop us in our tracks. We hear about one disaster after another, day in day out and then, very quickly, we forget. But you might still remember a few figures about the *Joola.* Originally built for 500 passengers, according to official reports, this ship was carrying 1,220. Or perhaps even as many as 2,000 if we believe the information the press has never refuted. The Commission of Inquiry reported 65 survivors – a miracle of course. With these figures, it is easy to make some calculations. No one here can bring himself to do this, of course, out of fear of having to face the terrible truth. The exact number of victims of this shipwreck is not just a State secret, it is a taboo.

It is true that this is of little importance to the hundreds of thousands of Senegalese citizens who have lost members of their immediate or extended families. I know what I am talking about. I am sure you remember young Hyacinthe Sagna who was living with us. He made you revisit Gorée Island last June and with his help, you had a lot of fun bargaining at Sandaga without doing too much damage to your bank balance. He was coming back from Ziguinchor with his brother Édouard and the moment I heard the news on the radio, I went to look for them. I could not find their names on any of the lists of survivors displayed in the hospitals and outside the town halls. But I saw horrific pictures: the bloated, puffed-up faces of about 20 victims, round like the moon, but distorted. One young woman in the crowd suddenly cried out – she had just discovered her husband. As she was weeping, we all looked at her with a certain envy. At least she had found a body to which she could attach her pain. She was lucky; it was a lot better to be in her shoes than being faced with nothing. The experience made me realize how very hard it is to accept the total disappearance, the sudden absence without a trace of someone we have known well and loved. I still can't bear the idea that Hyacinthe Sagna has somehow just disintegrated. Even now, three months after the tragedy, bodies are still being washed up and I am bewildered when I catch myself wishing that his should be one of them, so that his short life will at least not have been an adventure with no proper end.

The relatives of the victims in particular would have preferred never to hear about that night of horror. Under normal circumstances, when people have died a violent death, one doesn't discuss it. In the case of those who perished on the *Joola,* we know about their last moments in great detail. We know, for example, that they saw death closing in on them for an entire night, or that a certain young man was so exhausted he just gave up rather than continuing to swim. Women and children paid the highest tribute to the ocean and right now, as I am writing these lines, bodies are still trapped inside the ship in the most horrific manner; tormented by fear and a frantic hope against hope, the shipwrecked kept banging their fists against the hull until their final breath. It was in vain, since the rescuers who should have saved them were sleeping the sleep of the just.

The worst part may well be what we will never know.

Hyacinthe was a fervent catholic and his faith must have been a great source of strength to him. Other, spiritually less well-shielded passengers on the ship, may have felt like they were suddenly being thrown into Hell. It is simply awful to think that one of your loved ones, with terror in his eyes, has had all that time to wonder who had condemned him to such a gruesome death, who had accused him and of what? And yet, that is the lot of many of the victims' relatives. Each one of them is forced to relive the last moments of his daughter, his father or of his fiancée.

Diadié, a small phrase in your letter made me smile, but it was a smile filled with embarrassment and irritation. What you write is this, "I thought that something like this could happen anywhere in Africa, except in Senegal."

Without knowing it, you really have twisted the knife in our wound. For us, too, such things only used to happen to others. You know very well that modesty has never been our most outstanding characteristic. There is nothing wrong with a country which believes in its abilities, or which even overestimates them a little bit. But one must not overdo it. We had been deluding ourselves for too long and now there has been a brutal awakening.

This is why we didn't only ask our former president to let himself be beaten in the elections on March 19, 2000, but we also expected him to be graceful in defeat. This basically means that our people wanted to win twice, once with the winner and a second time with the loser. Diouf magnanimously played along with this callous game. His famous phone call to M. Wade – acknowledging his victory before the official results were even published and congratulating him – was more important for its democratic stance than its content. He allowed us to say to the world: aren't we Senegalese simply marvellous?

On the occasion of Senghor's funeral, less than a year later, we found ourselves at the centre of attention again in a very flattering way. Everybody remembered the first president of our country – which somehow defies classification – as a man of undeniable intellectual stature, no matter how ambiguous the role he played as a politician may have been. His voluntary resignation from power earned him additional respect.

Do I have to remind you how nothing has made us lose our head quite like our sporting exploits in Asia? The opening match of a world championship is something really unique. One could describe it as a duel, or single combat. In the one that pitted us against France, the entire planet played referee. A strange place all the same for an encounter between the former colonizer and us. This victory made me go absolutely crazy with joy! I bought flags for dozens of compatriots in Paris, in Boulogne and elsewhere. I had never been so proud of belonging to this nation, which is nevertheless a little bit odd. How does a country where soccer *had not existed* for decades, manage to first beat the World- and the European champion, then a whole lot of other national soccer teams? For nearly an entire month, we gave long shouts of joy every morning at dawn. Our new president had promised us happiness.

Clearly, our athletic successes were the harbingers of a brighter future! For M. Wade, this was never in doubt; with him at the helm of Senegal, there would be miracles aplenty, we just had to wait and see! And at precisely that moment, he started to become decidedly cranky, going through a rather unusual ritual for a Head of State after an election victory. He would become extremely emotional in public, gesticulating wildly and with a mad look in his eye and that among large crowds of his overexcited great grandchildren. So we have seen him ringing our soccer team in Seoul, not from the presidential palace but from a street-corner in Dakar, sending them his very cordial intercontinental greetings.

The president was certainly present on all fronts and nothing was too much for him. In fact, it was as if we had won the lottery. He was going to make our wildest dreams come true. Never has a poor country been so rich in future airports, motorways and universities and other projects of colossal proportions. There was just one small problem: it all only existed in his imagination. Encouraged by the Soccer World Cup, nothing would hold us back now. When unpatriotic people were talking about a drought, experts were called in from Morocco to shut them up. In between the clouds, they made us look at complicated diagrams which at the push of a button, would produce artificial rain in abundance. And because the reality was that the country was short of water, the television channels unleashed veritable tropical thunderstorms by using material stored in their archives.

Nobody was fooled, but the strategy worked brilliantly. And there was no reason why this should not have continued for a long time. We have always felt that magically somehow, we could escape the worst. The sinking of the *Joola* put a sudden stop to these absurd hallucinations. That was crystal clear on M. Wade's return from the francophone summit in Beirut. He portrayed the election of Diouf as head of the OIF[90] as a victory. "This, too," he said, "is a triumph for Senegal!" But one could see that his heart was no longer in it. His voice was a bit weary and he had lost the sparkle in his eye, our president. And anyway, it is well known that it wasn't out of the kindness of his heart that he supported Diouf 's candidacy for a post which was likely to reposition him, via a circuitous route, in a complex political game. But there was also another reason for the president's distress. He was very aware of the anger and hurt of his people because of the ferry disaster. To us, his grandiose phrases sounded like pathetic patriotic trivialities. Yes dear Dadié, we were beginning to ask ourselves whether we had not put the leadership into dangerously inexperienced hands, just for the sake of a change. The man who had promised us economic growth of goodness knows how many digits, only knew how to build makeshift cemeteries between Mbao, Ziguinchor and Banjul. It was distressing for us to see him, all by himself and trying to deal with hundreds of bodies that had hastily been thrown into containers. Never had the discrepancy between our fantasies and reality seemed more obvious. And what is there to say about the mistakes that prevented so many human lives from being saved? The ferry disaster took place at 11:00 pm in an area where the rebellion of the MFCD[91] had been raging for twenty years. Until 8 o'clock the next morning, no civil or military authority could be contacted. It is true that the Minister of Fisheries was informed during the night. Later, he innocuously said that he had not been able to do anything since he didn't have the mobile telephone number of his colleague in the Ministry of Transport! He didn't say so, but one knew anyway that he immediately went back to sleep, which is human, of course. This was a situation which was anything but funny, but where you often almost had to laugh. Two members of the government who will eventually be dismissed, kept passing the buck to each other for several days, while planning at the same time to blame the army.

And as for the army itself, it has been attacked with amazing vehemence. In Senegal, that is something new and deserves contemplation. We have always had the greatest respect for our army because there was never any grappling for power with civilians. And we love to believe – out of naivety or lack of information? – that for more than twenty years, our army has managed to avoid the frequent excesses so often seen in other countries which usually occur when the regular Armed Forces have to fight guerrillas. The catastrophe has demonstrated that our army has worrying problems to contend with in its own ranks. It has also cast a shadow over its reputation for discipline and professionalism that enabled it to be part of virtually all the UN peace missions. In one single night, the dereliction of duty of the commanders has caused more victims than years of regional wars of independence. Yesterday, the victims' families self – help group decided to demand the dismissal of the army's Chief-of-Staff.

Right from the start, president Wade admitted that the *Joola* disaster was not an act of God. Instead of blaming the natural elements, he has invited the Senegalese people to examine their conscience. "You are greedy," he shouted at us, "and you have no respect for the lives of others, shame on you!" And – would you believe it, dear friend? – despite the pain and the rage, we felt a shiver of contentment. I don't know if this political category makes any sense, but I would like to christen this reverse populism. We wanted to be told off and our venerable president, so attentive to our smallest desires, certainly fulfilled our expectations. Our people are generally so prone to blowing their own trumpet for no reason, but the tragedy of the 26th of September has taught them the virtues of collective self-flagellation. The way they indulged in it was maybe over the top, but it was apparently perfectly sincere. In reality, though, our dominant sentiment in the aftermath of this disaster was shame. When you are convinced you are skimming the clouds, it is not easy to admit to yourself that, like so many others, you are actually walking along the edge of an abyss. The defects our democracy was hiding under its glowing façade are very common, but they led to tragic consequences. The *Joola* has not only tarnished the image built on some of our true achievements; it has robbed us of the ability enjoy them and all we have left is a bitter taste. Without El Hadj Diouf's bizarre antics on the Asian soccer fields, this disaster would most probably have hurt us slightly less. By using and abusing the slogan 'Senegal is on a winning streak', we forgot to think about the backlash. We didn't know we were about to accomplish another feat by beating, with our one and only ship, the record set by the *Titanic.*

The image of the aeroplanes crashing into the Twin Towers will remain indelibly stamped on that fateful day, September 11, 2001. The tragedy that *we* will always remember is associated with those fishing-boats, visible just off the Isle of Karabane, circling the ship that was already tilting dangerously and trying to cram it with even more goods and passengers. It is raining on Karabane and the amateur video clips are all the more striking since they are blurred and shaky. It felt like the heart of darkness, one might say. A woman, totally drenched by the rain, is crossing a veranda that is strangely reminiscent of the jungle. Then she disappears in a flash, as though suddenly swallowed by the gloom, before one could even ask what she was doing there. But when death is on the prowl, such questions are pointless, because there are no answers, except that this shipwreck, which was predictable because there were warning signs, will be remembered as yet another African calamity. Or, to be more exact, as a colossal natural catastrophe, caused by human error. The deaths of hundreds of soldiers, merchants and above all students – the future of an entire region and of our country – had one reason and one reason alone, and that is the unfathomable incompetence of our leaders.

Afterwards, we spent a few days pretending that the event had taught us a lesson. I repeatedly saw policemen, with an ostentation that was slightly comical, standing at the city crossroads and checking the papers of the combi drivers, their former cronies. They seemed to be saying: "Sorry pal, but we're gonna have to stop our little game for a few days, there's been this accident at sea, the Prez says it's our bloody fault and now everybody's watchin' us. Don't ya listen to the news?" Then, at the back, a devious little wink, so easy to decipher: "Let's give all these lesson givers the chance to change the record! They're all crooks, with their four-by-fours and their beautiful ladies, we're just the small fry and now they're giving us a hard time, hey!" And since the press has been pointing out for years that Dakar is literally sitting on a time bomb, the ministers took a little tour around the industrial zone to confirm what they already knew. If one can be so bold as to talk about the Wadian method, it can be summed up as follows: react every time to give the impression of acting all of the time. In this particular case, the whole hullabaloo was punctuated by tiresome pontifications of the 'never again' variety from the authorities. The shock has been so severe that nobody suspects us of putting on an act, I think. And yet, all this contrition, so self-indulgently splashed out all over the newspaper columns bothers me, since it seems so superficial. Once we've calmed down again, the various different practices and procedures that made the sinking of the *Joola* possible will start blossoming again. You merely have to go for a walk anywhere in the capital and you will notice that things are exactly as they used to be before September 26, 2002.

I also believe, my dear Diadié, that our President is a lot like us. I think he must often be quite exasperated by the shocking state of our under-developed country which never seems to change. I was always convinced that he really wants to do a better job than his two predecessors. In some respects, he reminds me of Césaire's King Christophe – "What I demand from mankind is huge! But from the negroes I am not asking enough, Madam! […] I am talking about an increase like the world has never seen it before, Gentlemen and woe betide anyone who gets cold feet". He reminds me even more of Haroun al-Rashid, the caliph in the *Arabian Nights* who waits until his faithful subjects in Baghdad are asleep before putting on a foreign merchant's cloak and checking that everything in his kingdom is, as Sheherazade says, 'in apple-pie order.' I could very well imagine M. Wade doing just that, sneaking into some dark alleyway in Colobane when everybody else is tucked up in bed. When he comes across a broken traffic light, he feverishly notes it down; a whole family of beggars is huddled up on pieces of cardboard near a rubbish dump and the president is scratching his head, wondering…A ministry for the Fight against Extreme Poverty, wouldn't that be the best solution? He is going to talk about it in his speech the following day but his next nocturnal stroll will make the presidential interest veer off in another direction. And thus, the eternal round of ideas that come and go will continue until the cows come home.

I am telling you exactly what I think, Diadié. Due to his futile desire to be everywhere, M. Wade confuses and aggravates our problems without solving them. One could probably say that we have moved on from the inertia of Diouf's final years to a frenetic activism which, at the end of the day, is no less paralyzing. Today, all the ministers are so petrified that they are trying to hide and seem to be saying; "Don't pay any attention to me. Perhaps you can see me in the flesh, but that's a mistake, I'm not here." With a man like that, it is probably wiser to prove at all times that you don't exist. You never know. Maybe we should whisper in our president's ear that we do not think he is superhuman, but we are just pretending to give him courage for his task. We should tell him that right from the start we have been expecting a move in the right direction from him and not conjuring tricks. If it is possible to really learn from this tragedy, it must be to understand that a true democracy has no use for a man who feels he is a gift from heaven. A country cannot remain in suspended animation, holding its breath because of the alleged or real superior insight of a single human being. That has a stultifying effect and could cause us to meet with a truly calamitous fate one day with our hands and feet in fetters.

We have all been asked to examine our conscience. Very well. I just think it would be fairer to hold only the decision makers responsible. The disaster happened at a specific time, under circumstances which have been described in detail in the report drawn up by the Commission of Inquiry. To accuse everybody in this quasi-metaphysical manner is simply a way of circumventing a clear attribution of the blame. It is not so much a matter of making heads roll as of preventing a dangerous culture of impunity. At the same time, to do M. Wade justice, we have to point out that he did not hesitate to get rid of several close staff members who were indicted for dubious trafficking. What we don't know, of course, is whether he will take these salutary disciplinary measures to their logical conclusion.

The tragedy of the 26th of September was so grave that this time, our politicians should not count on their closest ally: our short memory. And then, every time we think it's finally over, the *Joola* is spewing bodies onto the beaches again. For the victims, this is a way of turning their death into a gift for us, as though they wanted to remind us of our duty to keep their memory alive.

Yet I have my doubts, Diadié. Call me a pessimist again, but I am telling you that the screams of the survivors and the victims' families are fading away. You know what? The report on the sinking of the *Joola* was made public on the same day as a cabinet reshuffle that was bristling with suspense and widely publicized in the media.

Which one of the two events, do you think, has eclipsed the other? Even our beloved Niouma Dagnoko, whom I sincerely wish to see living in a better world than ours, knows the answer...

And now for the quick little wink that habitually closes all our letters and for which we have conveniently invented the word 'flashback.' Undoubtedly, you remember the day when, in Mopti, the Master told us the following: "If the king becomes a murderer, both he and his subjects should share the guilt. But if a murderer becomes king, the people who have allowed him to usurp the throne have no one to blame but themselves." Has anybody ever expressed more clearly and yet indirectly, what the problem is with sinking ships and sinking nations, Diadié? Isn't he a funny man, the Master – immensely wise and a bit crazy, which I guess is quite normal for an aspiring philosopher.

Looking forward to our next encounter, either here or over there, I remain, with my best wishes to my companions-in-hope at Bamako.

SECTION III

African Literature: Words versus things

Write and...Keep Quiet

African authors, especially those who are francophone, spend most of their time explaining why they are writing in a foreign language. This frequently makes them feel frustrated and trapped in a pointless discussion. The Congolese poet Tchicaya U Tam'si once explained how very fed up he was with this ongoing debate. There is also the story that Mongo Beti was so exasperated that he told a lady in his audience: "Madam, I detest the French language, I actually only like Greek and Latin!" For decades now, the same questions have been eliciting the same answers: our audience, more receptive to the spoken than the written word, also lacks the means to buy or understand our books.

However, apart from a few exceptions like the Kenyan Ngugi wa Thiong'o and Cheik Aliou Ndao from Senegal, for example, most African authors prefer not to write in their mother tongue, even if they could. It is probably fair to say that they consider English or French as the lesser evil; their attitude is simply an expression of their legitimate fear of being locked into a ghetto which might isolate them from the rest of humanity. As a matter of fact, one cannot really blame a poet or a playwright for wanting to spread his or her ideas beyond his or her native community. Common sense demands that s/he should address all potential readers, no matter where on earth they might be. Sony Lab'ou Tansi put the same idea into his own words, "I write for the whole world and not just for the Congolese."

While such a proposition is of course plausible, one is nevertheless struck by the refusal it implies to establish any link whatsoever between language and culture. And this is all the more surprising since in other parts of the world, the language question has always been at the heart of the identity issue, occasionally even leading to bloodshed. Curiously, in Africa, language does not indicate an ideological split in the field of literature.[92] Novelists who are totally opposed to each other in every other way agree entirely on this point. For them, moving away from the *dioula* or *serer* idiom does not signify a denial of their African identity. It sometimes even looks as though the most anti-colonial authors mind this state of affairs the least.

This may seem paradoxical, but isn't, since the African artist has two audiences. He is at least as eager to be heard by the oppressor as he is to improve the lot of his compatriots. Born as a vehicle of collective protest, African literature has always been wary of 'Art for Art's sake.' Our writers are less interested in the creation of individual works of beauty than in discussing urgent social problems and how to solve them. During the period of the national liberation struggle, it was necessary to concentrate on the most pressing issues. The language of the invader had the merit of existing and African intellectuals extracted *passwords* from it, which ensured their unity in the face of a common enemy.

However, the situation is not the same in all the former colonies. In the anglophone parts of the continent the only thing that renders the language debate even remotely realistic is Ngugi wa Thiong'o's determination. In Nigeria, the writings of Wole Soyinka live easily side by side with works in Yoruba or Hausa. According to certain analysts, this more laid back attitude is due to the fact that on close scrutiny, the British occupation has proved less destructive for the African elites. And besides, people often say that the English language has conquered the planet. Shouldn't one rather say that it has been colonized by the other cultures? It is perfectly possible that Ben Okri and Arundhati Roy consider it as their personal property. The supremacy of the English language bothers no one except the French, who have an almost neurotic relationship with their own language and the fact that the relevance of the latter is fading certainly doesn't improve things. What is known as 'francophony' is a rather ludicrous way for the French to try and impress their eternal Anglo-Saxon rival. By laying claim to all the francophone authors from around the world, France primarily wants to demonstrate its global reach and the enduring vitality of its language. This way, France can at least perpetuate the illusion that it has 'kept its position' among the great nations of the world. But this apparent openness is deceptive, since the French literary establishment is encouraging authors from Quebec, Lebanon, Switzerland or Ivory Coast to compete with each other, without being able to make up its mind to treat them and writers from the Hexagon itself as equals. Due to a strange semantic shift, we are now in a situation where a French writer would feel discredited if he was called francophone...How bewildering!

People from Quebec and the French speakers from Belgium and Switzerland can claim to be part of a French culture which has its common roots in a past which is, at times, fairly recent. It is quite different for Africans, since the place they are occupying in this extremely diverse family is essentially political. The reason they are staying there is twofold: to boost the numbers and because their leaders do not dare to displease Paris. And yet, so much should be pushing them away from the francophone community: the geography, their painful past, the economic situation, the different way of life and even... the language!

This becomes even clearer if one considers the act of writing from within. The Swiss author Yves Laplace composes his books in a language which he speaks and hears all around him every day. It is an important part of his culture. The Bamanan that the Malian Moussa Konaté speaks at home, on the other hand, has nothing in common with the French he uses in his novels. This means that the realms of the written- and the spoken word are totally out of step, which must be unique in the world and is bound to affect the relationship between the African author and his imagination, as well as his writing. If he is not able to put either all of the material world around him, or certain specific cultural traits, into words, it makes him feel that silence has gained the upper hand over his verbal power. The fact that his words don't always obey him may make his style rather clumsy. A borrowed word means an awkward word and when it is remembered, it is full of holes! This last point is vital: it explains, perhaps, why what we write, even when it is supposed to be funny, always sounds so grave and serious. One might even ask oneself whether we are working with a dead language which does not exist anywhere anymore, since its vocabulary and syntax have barely evolved, particularly in the cities. Just a little stroll in the exuberant, colourful and noisy streets of Yaounde or Kinshasa immediately brings home the contrast between real life and our works of fiction which are supposed to describe it. The world they talk about doesn't resemble ours.

In order to deal with this problem, Massa Makan Diabaté advocated 'the creation of hybrids of the French language.' Ahmadou Kourouma, for instance, rejected grammatical norms he found too cumbersome and invented his own French, suffused and enriched with the rhythms and sounds of his vernacular Malinké. Although what he did was generally well received, it is still a questionable approach. In an interview with the Dakar daily *Le*

Matin, Cheikh Hamidou Kane made his position clear when he said, "I disagree with my friend Kourouma; when you use French in order to write in French, it has to be done correctly." While certainly paying the author of *The Suns of Independence* his due, a number of his fellow authors expressed similar reservations, but less politely.

Faced with the champions of a purely classical style, the refusal to submit to any sort of restriction may seem innovative, or even subversive. But this is not the case. In fact, 'the Kourouma model' was born out of inadequacy. It basically means that Malinké ought to die – rot? – inside the French language and that French is not just a tool that history has *temporarily* imposed upon us, but that we are stuck with it forever. Every nation has enough problems to deal with. It is quite possible that the language of Molière is in need of a little shake-up. And then? That doesn't concern us in the slightest, of course. That is really not going to be our problem, but the French writers will have to deal with it. What matters is positioning the language issue at the heart of the debate about the future of African societies. From that perspective, it is a better idea to take one's inspiration from Cheikh Anta Diop rather than Kourouma.

Insofar as the creation of literature is concerned, what matters at the end of the day are the insights born out of our unique life experience and our most intensely personal emotions. When an author is too concerned about the reception of his text, he is in danger of losing out on the simple pleasure of writing. Every author is entitled to listen exclusively to his inspiration of the moment. Even if the young novelists – Kossi Efoui and Daniel Biyaoula among others – are insisting more and more fervently on creative freedom as their birthright, our literature remains dependent on its original political ideas and intentions. The African author, who is quick to hide behind his audience, does not find it easy to lock himself into his 'I'. That is probably why our literary output is almost entirely restricted to fiction. It lacks the kind of 'periphery' that in the older literary canons comprises correspondence between writers, personal journals, memoirs, essays or confessions. One frequently does not know much about what sort of relationship the writer has with reality, what he thinks about the underlying concept of his work, or about the difference between the text he ended up writing and the one he carried in his head at the beginning. Very rarely does he feel the need to make spontaneous comments about the technicalities of his fiction. It is far more likely that he is approached by an outsider who asks him questions. He will answer with a great deal of good will, even if he contradicts himself once in a while. Basically, one can describe this situation by saying that the African author almost always has a spokesperson who speaks on is behalf, but is telling him, in a harsh, commanding tone: *write....and keep quiet!*

To see oneself as a unique voice is not wanting to stand out from the rest, but rather to seek one's inspiration from the well-spring of all art. Fiction is an act of rupture, in that it brings the conflicts and failures of a social group to the surface, rather than trying to conceal them. The writer is, by definition, a traitor. That also means he is a being of pure love.

I would like to explain why, after having published my previous books in a foreign language, I decided to also write in Wolof from then on. For the past twenty years, French has never been a problem for me at all. It has always been an acceptable option for me and I never had the feeling that it was a vantage point that alienated me from my African roots.

I want to state clearly that my attitude would have been exactly the same even if I hadn't taken such a strong interest in the Rwandan Genocide of 1994.

The principal conclusion I have drawn from the Rwandan tragedy, as I explained in a previous chapter of this book, is that it was largely the result of the French government's desire to preserve its sphere of influence in Africa South of the Sahara. In addition, hundreds and thousands of people lost their lives in Rwanda because of France's determination not to give up a francophone stronghold which was supposed to be 'under threat' by the anglophone enemy who had come in from Uganda. What's more, the interpretation of the Rwandan Genocide by certain intellectuals and influential French politicians has been, in my opinion, an absolute disgrace. Offensive statements have shamelessly been splashed across the pages in the Western press. This denigration then gathered momentum and started to spread to the rest of Africa. And now, we are starting to read that colonization was, despite everything else that may have been said, nothing but a 'voluntary servitude.'[93]

Racism is alive and well, but a few years ago it still used to be practised with a bit more tact. Now, the statements are crystal clear: those who died in 1994 don't count because they were black. Such an utterance forces you to look at yourself more carefully in the mirror. After all, my country, Senegal, entertains a relationship with France which calls itself cooperation, but which is in fact a neo-colonial relationship and therefore identical to that which caused Paris to compromise itself so gravely in its involvement with the butchers of Kigali and elsewhere.

To write in Wolof is a way of taking shelter from all this nastiness and filth and putting one's feet on firm and reassuring ground. In some sense, the vicissitudes of a dangerous world lead us all back to where we feel safe. Seeking to improve the literary standing of African languages is not a rear guard action, but on the contrary the way into the future. We probably don't point it out enough, but for entire nations, the disconnection between language and culture is a perilous situation to be in. Far too many of the ex-colonized are now dreaming of becoming the other. I am not sure about the rest of Africa, but in Senegal, where the national languages are fortunately not under any threat, you quite often come across educated couples who do not allow their children to speak any other language except French. In certain private schools the regulations are still exactly the same as during the colonial era.

I have been able to resort to Wolof, but I am aware that not all African writers have this luxury. Their native tongues may not have been codified or they may not have studied them, either at university or elsewhere. Mine has, since the 19th century, had its own literature, initially using Arabic characters, but later changing to the Roman alphabet. The poem by Seriñ Muusaa Ka, *Xarnu bi* – "The century" – for example, deals with the consequences of the 1929 economic crisis in his native Baol…

The fact that I have changed my linguistic practices clearly came as a surprise to some of my friends. The reactions I have observed range from slight discomfort to frank hostility and resentment. For them, such a lunatic decision incurs too many losses at the same time: audience, prestige and even the little bit of money one can expect to get out of a literary career. I have, however, never declared that I have stopped publishing novels in French.

Any language, even if it has been learnt under duress, will enrich us in the end. It would therefore be stupid to go to war against just anybody. I was reminded of the examples of Ngugi wa Thiong'o, Rachid Boudjedra and Raphaël Confiant who would not have been able to stick to the commitment of only writing in Gikuyu, Arabic or Creole, from one day to the next. I have had to respond to a few amusing questions which were very revealing. Does Wolof have verbs? Do you write it from left to right or vice versa?

All this has helped me understand that not many people, either in Africa or in the West, believe that African languages are capable of expressing an inner world in the appropriate way. Maybe I myself had the same doubts without being bold enough to admit it. The truth is that we have been so deeply alienated that we need courage and a bit of madness to come back to ourselves. But anyone who takes that leap of faith will be hugely rewarded, since – I have seen it myself – writing in your mother tongue makes you experience feelings which you would have thought absolutely impossible before.

And what about the fact that our languages play such an insignificant role internationally? We are simply going wrong in trying to apply standards to African literature which are totally foreign to it. So far, we have no conclusive proof that a novel in Pulaar or in Swahili has no audience. The available statistics show the exact opposite. But even if we assume that this is so, it is common knowledge that initially, every literature has to go through a long and painful birth process. Centuries or even millennia are required before it is properly established. In this light, Franco-African literature may well only represent a brief period of transition in a more complex historical trajectory. The act of writing in our languages by itself is not enough and a lot of time has been wasted. To catch up will not be an easy task but this is the price we have to pay for our alienation. Generally, the role of the writer is not to tell his readers what they ought to think or do, but, much more modestly, to talk about himself, through his fantasies, in many cases. An author not only uses language, but he also creates it, thus promoting social change. When I write in Wolof, more than anything, it makes me feel that I am taking my place in an emerging national literature.

And when I compare my earlier novels to *Doomi Golo,* I realize now that the words of 'the Other' helped me articulate as much as they reduced me to silence or a pathetic stammer. It always gives me deep satisfaction when I remind people that I never speak French in everyday life. That would make absolutely no sense in the society I live in. For me, French is a language for special occasions, my Sunday language, as it were. I am in the process of discovering that in literature, the meaning is entirely locked up in the echo, in the pure resonance of words. The words I use to write *Doomi Golo* do not come from school or from a dictionary. They come from real life. These words rise up to me from a very distant past, and if their sound is simultaneously so familiar and so pleasing to me, it is because I belong, with every fibre of my being to an oral tradition.

Never before has my childhood been so naturally present in my fiction. Sometimes I ask myself whether a trick of the subconscious is making me do this, allowing me to hear again the voice of my mother who has been dead several years, or those of other people whose existence I had completely forgotten. All I can say is that these voices are emerging from secret places where they have lain dormant for aeons, hoping to be given a second life that will last forever.

Mongo Beti and Us

During the seventies, the smartest, trendiest leftist thing to do at Dakar University was to walk around the campus, clutching certain books for everyone to see. It was the heyday of the Maspero editions and the students' favourites obviously included the writings of Frantz Fanon, Cheikh Anta Diop, Mao Tse-Tung and Amilcar Cabral and others who were never mentioned in the lecture theatres. The professors were talking erudite drivel about *Force-Bonté* or *The Twilight of the Bygone Days*, while we were listening with one ear and daydreaming. Mongo Beti, already famous by then, was on the syllabus. Initially, we saw him as a writer like all the others, mainly because our professors were so versed in the art of bringing everything down to the same common denominator. All the set books of fiction on the reading list had had their special features rubbed out of them in advance. In this semantic hotchpotch, it was easy to pass off tedious authors as formidable enemies of the colonial order. On the other hand, works as powerful as *The Poor Christ of Bomba* or *Mission to Kala* literally passed us by. Perhaps we did sense a different vibe in the sarcasm of these novels, but that's how far it went. Dead keen on simple ideas and brutal solutions as we were, we couldn't really fathom them. We were just young and hot-headed and some of us perhaps even suspected Beti of being too 'petit-bourgeois' as a writer.

But the publication of *Cruel Hand on Cameroon* in 1972 changed our opinion of Mongo Beti radically and permanently. One can easily imagine that the immediate censoring of this satire by neo-colonial France could only have added to the aura of its author. With his habitual caustic brilliance, he himself said afterwards about this work that he was describing 'the atmosphere in a former French colony which had become a French colony all over again.' And that was exactly our perception at the time, so much so that we circulated the book from hand to hand and had heated discussions about it in our study groups. In it and based on the special situation in Cameroon, Beti voiced his opinion on the major political issues and we were very well aware that he was risking his life in doing so. Like Fanon and Césaire, he was one of the thinkers who helped us to a better understanding of the causes and mechanisms of our alienation. By showing us a true life path, he removed us from the sugary fairy tales of some of the fashionable scribblers. It's true that they were sometimes quite amusing, but they simply couldn't be taken seriously. We immediately started to re-read his entire oeuvre in a new light. The publication of each one of Beti's texts gradually turned into a sort of political event. His fame was not limited to the department of literature, far from it. It was not unusual to come across a medical student engrossed in the dissection of Banda's state of mind in *Cruel City,* or making fun of the tyrant Ahidjo, alias Baba Toura. To some extent, the battle for the lifting of the ban on *Cruel Hand on Cameroon* was also ours. This is reflected in some of our declarations, in-between hard-hitting insults aimed at Jacques Foccart and the rather childish threat of blowing up French military bases in Africa.

If it is true that a writer is always identified with only one of his books, Beti will definitely remain, for a number of African intellectuals, the author of the provocative work that has familiarised us with the battle of the UPC and the names of Osendé Afana, Félix-Roland Moumié and Ruben Um Nyobé. In a certain way, we can define ourselves as the generation that has read *Cruel Hand on Cameroon.*

Having initially travelled along the wrong path in his literary world led us to the discovery of the other face of this African writer, radically different from the idea we had of him until then. Beti was averse to compromise and always able to say: 'I don't agree'. Such simple words, but not often heard. The ease with which he managed to confuse impostors, both in the realm of literature and elsewhere, was, and still is today, quite exceptional. He is thus the only person to have had the courage to say publicly what he really thought of Camara Laye or Ahmadou Kourouma. And his magazine *Black People, African People,* founded in 1978, was not flattering to certain mediocre authors who had been praised to the high heavens by cynical kingmakers.

Besides their strange titles, one is struck by the jubilant frenzy of novels like *Too Much Sun Kills Love* and *Turmoil in White and Black.* After fourteen years of silence between *King Lazarus* and *Cruel Hand on Cameroon,* he perhaps felt like having a go at literature itself. His latest texts however, give the impression that he had come full circle; one feels that it was a time when Mongo Beti was rediscovering the joy of writing of his younger years, some bitterness and his desire to create havoc thrown in for good measure. It is also true that towards the end of his life he often stated that he believed more in direct political action than in the power of the pen. Convinced as he was that he should rather defend his ideas in Parliament than by writing fiction or essays, he even allowed his name to be put on a candidate list. And when *Cruel Hand on Cameroon* was banned, he conned the censors by making the subject matter reappear in *Perpetua* and *Remember Ruben*, both of which were published in 1974. This shows that literature for him was not just a game, an easy way of elevating himself to the status of intellectual before joining in the dance of servitude. One of his compatriots to whom he is unfortunately often compared and whom he despised, was an expert in this dubious practice. But this genuine author really only was who he was because he abhorred professional writers, their affectations and their stereotypes. If Africa has never lacked theorists, particularly during the era of the national liberation struggles, he, together with the Kenyan Ngugi wa Thiong'o, was one of the very few who fully realized their double vocation as novelists and political thinkers. Through all his novels, essays and outspoken statements, Beti became for us the embodiment of the liberal intellectual, someone who was prepared to pay for his convictions, recognizing no master other than his own conscience and always expecting at least as much of himself as of others. But today, one would have to admit that our history with him wasn't always pure perfection. Mongo Beti was probably quite alone for a number of years. When his erstwhile admirers had grown up they continued to respect him as an important writer, but not without distancing themselves from his fight against *Françafrique.* This near-rift is best explained as being quite simply caused by a certain disaffection for ideological debate and by everybody's desire to at last find their place in the sun. You can also call it settling down. For some of us, however, things weren't quite so easy. It may be that, quite against our will, we had become floating, fuzzy creatures, a bit like the tormented heroes of Sassine and Mudimbé. It was just that we were no longer for or against anything; despair had become our *raison d'être* and this extraordinary mental confusion had made it impossible for us to perceive the clarity of Mongo Beti's words. At many African writers' conferences, rather nasty things were being whispered about the Cameroonian author. The young and the not so young criticized him for being so uncompromisingly harsh towards others, but totally forgetting that he was often even harder on himself. It was easy to see that even while he was absent, the shadowy and solitary Beti continued to be our guilty conscience.

We could neither hate nor despise him. The truth is that above all, he made us afraid. On occasion, someone was clear-headed enough to exclaim with admiration and a touch of envy: "What a man he is, despite everything! His tantrums haven't stopped for forty years!" Eternal iconoclast that he was, he was really always younger than his juniors. The main accusation levelled at him by his opponents was that he claimed he was influencing the situation in his native country while actually living in France, out of the firing line of all the calamities. And then he went and took the wind out of their sails by deciding one day in 1994 to return to Yaoundé for good, after forty-two years in exile. Besides the fact that he simply ignored the dangers it involved, the moral value of this homecoming consists mainly in his desire to follow up his ideas with action. It was not out of bloody-mindedness at the time that he refused to follow his friends' advice to be careful, but rather because he had the feeling that he could be useful on the spot. Nobody thought it even remotely possible that this fierce political opponent could enter into any sort of relationship with the ignominious Paul Biya regime. What did not come as a surprise to anybody, however, was the exemplary manner and the total commitment with which he became involved in the struggle for democracy in Cameroon.

He had barely arrived when he opened what he referred to as 'the first real bookshop in Cameroon since independence' during a conversation with Alain Patrice Nganang. To be precise, it partly owed its success to the fact that he had the courage to sell the sort of political literature Cameroonians are so keen on and which nobody had dared to offer them. In 1997, Titus Edzoa, a former minister and Biya's personal physician, was thrown into prison without any form of trial. Beti, who had never met him, assembled a pressure group for his release. "It was a question of principle," he would say two years later, "I never set eyes on him, but each time there is an issue involving human rights, I stand up and protest." In November 1998, he launched *SOS-Libertés et Nature*, an association aimed at utilizing the exploitation of natural resources for the promotion of, and respect for, basic liberties. In keeping with his conviction that writers ought to be – in his own words – 'citizens of merit', he also fought for the rights of the peasants who had been robbed of their land. In February 2000, together with his wife Odile Tobner-Biyidi and a few friends – one of whom was Abel Eyinga – he set up a 'Committee for the repatriation of the public funds embezzled by Mr. Paul Biya for the benefit of a foreign religious sect.' The sums involved were estimated to be in the region of several billion Francs CFA.

The purpose of his stubborn presence on the social front is clear; by using his status as a writer, he wanted to support the development of a Cameroonian civil society capable of counterbalancing a totally ruinous dictatorship on the verge of insanity. And since he knew better than anyone that that sort of power had to be propped up by Paris, he saluted, in his own particular way, the twentieth anniversary of the accession to power of the French Left: "François Mitterrand's political programme in Africa," which he declared in May 2001 on an international radio channel, "was pure cynicism." That he never ceased to express his hatred of despotism and to castigate France's stranglehold over the continent is evident from his *Open Letter to the People of Cameroon*[94] and in 1993, *France against Africa, Return to Cameroon.*[95] And during the lawsuit against Xavier-François Verschave, he was there again, giving evidence in favour of the author of *Black Silence.*[96]

We have all read the brief and indignant replies of Odile Tobner-Biyidi to the hypocritical messages of condolence from Paul Biya and Ferdinand Oyono. The fact that they should have had the audacity to abuse the memory of a man of his stature, so soon after he had breathed his last, does not mean he was rejected by his own people, quite on the contrary. His own son Emmanuel-Alexandre, proud of a father "who was buried just like he lived, very modestly," says exactly that in an interview with the *Messenger*. And he added: "I was struck by the close ties he kept with some of his friends. This became obvious just before his death and also during the funeral." Those who came in order to snigger beside Beti's grave have nothing to do with the oppressed people of Cameroon he always loved and defended. Like his son, they could have said that he "sacrificed a lot, even everything, for Cameroon. One could even claim that he worked himself to death."

It has to be said that African literary circles reacted with a certain sense of embarrassment to Mongo Beti's death. Having acknowledged the importance of his oeuvre, they obviously understood the extraordinary singularity of this writer. For once, everybody went straight to the heart of the matter: despite the political intimidation and the social pressures, he managed to keep going until the end. All the intellectuals from poor countries know how very hard that is.

One must also ask, as does an article on October 10, 2001 in the daily *Cameroon Tribune*, why he has never received the kind of recognition his literary genius should have earned him. This is particularly surprising if one knows to what extent these forms of recognition can be manipulated. Yes, they require talent, but even more important is an excellent character. Quite a number of literary reputations in Africa, past and present, are built on repudiation and dishonesty, concealed behind the sanctimonious refusal to accept the established order. Mongo Beti never cared for the potential rewards of this kind of game. In the past, our kings allowed themselves to be enticed with glass beads before selling off their nations to the conqueror for next to nothing. The same procedure, under a different guise, continues to hold our intellectual and political elites captive. A brief fragment of a sentence coming from the mouth of the young Medza makes one think that Beti conceived his disdain for recognition very early. Surely that is what made him so unassailable. Together with Sembène Ousmane, Cheikh Anta Diop, Ayi Kwei Armah and a number of others, Beti expects us to write without ever giving in or bowing to anyone. He succeeded in doing this, turning a simple pseudonym into a rallying cry. Throughout his life, he hated hypocrisy, shallow fabrication and subterfuge. He remained faithful to his love of freedom and was prepared to sacrifice everything to it. At the final reckoning, what is left for those who, like us, have admired and feared him so much.... is a lesson in dignity. His death gives new significance to a full life. It anchors his political activism and his literary legacy in eternity. It also irrevocably establishes him as one of the points of reference of which we are going to be so greatly in need.

SECTION IV

Exchange to change our World

Carona

The Global Village

Carona, a tiny village in Italian-speaking Switzerland, is so landlocked that when I first arrived there, I was genuinely surprised to find a tobacconist with internet access. I used it extensively to check my emails, send messages to friends all over the world and read the Dakar newspapers online.

Afterwards, I went to look for a table at the *Ristorante della Posta*, just a few metres away from there. While I was waiting to be served, I noticed loud-speakers in two corners of the ceiling, broadcasting a musical programme on one of the local radio channels. I suddenly pricked up my ears, because I thought I had heard the announcer mentioning the name Youssou N'Dour. I was right – a few moments later, he started playing one of the Senegalese singer's recent compositions. At first, this amazing coincidence left me quite cold. But after a little while, it struck me that this was an unlikely place to be encountering my mother tongue. It was so strange to be hearing phrases in Wolof joyously colliding with the conversation in Italian of three other guests, middle-aged men in raptures about the exploits of Lazio Roma over their glass of white…

To think of Carona as a … global village after this was not such a big step and it was a step I was perfectly happy to take. And yet, I didn't want to jump to any conclusions. Surely you do not hear music from every corner of the world in Carona on a daily basis. And such easy Internet access in a village of five hundred souls in the canton of Ticino? It could just be the exception that proves the rule. So, even assuming that all this is slightly unusual, one still has to acknowledge that nowadays, these sorts of exceptions are *within the realm of the possible.* It is a sign of the times we live in and the inexorable progress which nobody and nothing will stop. These little interludes, somehow so "out of synch" with ordinary everyday life, are bringing us closer to the glittering world of our dreams, a world where diversity co-exists harmoniously with solidarity and where people from different backgrounds can rub shoulders without fear or favour. And yes, it wasn't difficult at all to strike up a conversation with the restaurant owner. Roberto – that was his name – had never set foot on the African continent and I had just arrived in Carona. So we had a lot to talk about. He told me the story of a pig named Charlie. Charlie was a bit like the village mascot. He used to wander around everywhere, enormous as he was, he weighed one- or two hundred kilos. He was the pride and joy of his owner, who had been given Charlie as a wedding present. But one night, a prankster stole the animal, 'turned him into Salami' – in Roberto's words – and then sent a letter to the local rag, the *Corriere del Ticino,* boasting about his wicked deed. It is simultaneously atrocious and hilarious, this story about Charlie. Ten years later, it still makes Roberto laugh, who rightly concludes by saying, "This is the kind of thing that can only happen in a small village."

At the tobacconists, things weren't quite so simple. The proprietor, originally from Zug, didn't speak a single word of French. Her painful efforts to come up with a few sentences which could build some sort of bridge between us, ended in failure and an apologetic shrug of her shoulders. I couldn't suppress a secret little smile – I wasn't surprised. After all, I was in Switzerland and nowhere else. Despite its large number of polyglots, one always has the impression that this is the only country in the world where every citizen lacks one or both of the other languages. The problem lies with their pretence to be trilingual, which in most cases they are not....

If language doesn't manage to divide people then technology will do it with ease and as so often in a destructive manner.

The internet is not only the most popular forum for the dissemination of racist and revisionist theories, it is also, slowly but surely, developing into the most modern way of not speaking. It is more and more common, it seems, in many different work environments, to contact the colleague sitting opposite you by email. Certain office workers are, as we all know, by nature very reserved. So who can blame them if they call the multimedia to their aid?

We also know that many people, when they get home after work, still can't take their eyes off the computer, and no longer find the time to talk to their partner or say hello to their neighbour. All they usually manage to do is utter a few exhausted grunts, begging their children to go and play somewhere else. It is much more important, of course, that they can think of themselves as constantly in touch with Karachi, São Paolo, San Francisco and other remote corners of the earth. Those in the know, however, are beginning to make fun of these internauts. Recent studies have shown that these people are completely deluded when they fancy themselves as intrepid adventurers. Some of these lounge-navigators rarely cross their national borders. The truth is that they mainly use the internet for shopping, accessing the weather forecast, or reading their favourite local papers.

That is exactly how I spent my first morning in Carona. I basically hadn't left my own country, its music and its political battles, all of them so intense and enigmatic at the same time, especially when you look at them from a distance. In a word, a trip around the world is no longer what it used to be; it will always take you back to your own doorstep...

Since today it is theoretically possible for every human being to find out so much information about other societies, encountering what is foreign to us should no longer pose a problem. The fact that this is not the case is therefore a bit worrying.

One possible solution, the most obvious one in fact, lies in cultural exchange, which represents an opportunity to enter into a continuing dialogue around and about the many differing ways of seeing the world and at the same time making the reassuring discovery that all these perspectives have a great deal in common. Between the nineteen sixties and the eighties, Senghor stubbornly upheld his conviction that the year 2000 would be, for every single nation on earth, the year of 'giving and receiving.' That was at a time when the intellectuals, particularly those in the developing countries, could not imagine globalization except in the form of the universal dictatorship of the proletariat. This great event never took place, just like the big universal banquet. A huge lesson in humility. All we need to do today is to determine who was more gravely mistaken – Senghor or his detractors. Even if there is no indication that we will be allowed a little respite from all the hatred, on balance, the poet may have been slightly more sensible. It is difficult, nowadays, to conceive of any way out of intolerance other than culture. Culture has become, somehow by default, the one and only response to the language of war. Culture is essentially democratic in the sense that the question whether a nation is rich or poor has next to no relevance. Culture is perhaps the last bastion of human activity where interpersonal relationships are still based on equality and mutual respect.

Exchange and direct contact go hand in hand. The circulation of cultural assets is entirely conditional upon the mobility of the artist, but this is not how everybody sees the situation.

For some time now, the northern countries have been eagerly voting for the type of politician for whom keeping out foreigners is at the top of his agenda. The typical xenophobe does not really resemble the caricature his opponents like to draw. He does not have angular features, a narrow forehead and a vicious gaze. He is much more terrifying, in that nothing distinguishes him from the ordinary man in the street. Each election reassures him again in his belief that he is only saying aloud what everybody is secretly thinking. He sees himself as a representative of the silent majority, the sort of people who are permanently gloomy and practically too scared to use the tram and the underground. At the same time he makes them laugh and stirs up their indignation with his tirades. His reasoning conforms perfectly to that of the arch-philistine at all times and he is not open to discussion, full stop. He thinks human solidarity is not a good enough reason for every nation to burden itself with financial difficulties. Pointing out to him that the Arts and Humanities are a vehicle of tolerance would be a waste of time. Without wanting to be accused of racism, he does not understand why we always insist on talking about culture with respect to absolutely anything and everything. And that the poor countries still find it within themselves to dance and laugh while they are so close to the abyss leaves him utterly perplexed. But that has nothing to do with him, of course; what he is worried about is that all these artists who get invited to Europe shouldn't push the spirit of friendship just a bit too far by refusing to go back home. Does he get castigated for that by the intellectuals? He couldn't care less. He just knows that he is engaged in a subtle role play. He has agreed to play the villain versus opponents who pride themselves on their open-mindedness. And the result? Everywhere in Europe, the immigration laws are increasingly in keeping with the views of right wing extremist politicians.

The thing is that in the South, one doesn't really know anymore which West one should trust – the one which opens its arms in a generous gesture of friendship or the one which closes its borders?

And this is not even the only reason why people are so bewildered, or indeed angry. Now that the Pandora's Box is open, it is frightening to see how much venom has accumulated over several centuries. The South has not completely lost its memory. In the past, the West had a lot of interest in its civilizations. That is what brought about colonization. But this colonization, as Césaire so rightly said, has not been an *encounter* so much as an extremely violent *shock* which caused a cultural cataclysm. Entire populations were slaughtered, deprived of their rights and alienated from their roots, as though it was nothing. They suffered such a profound upheaval that its effect still reverberates centuries later. And *à propos* cultural exchange, how can one forget that the treasures taken by force from the colonized are continuing to grace European museum walls today?

The sincerity of the champions of cultural diversity is not in doubt. But that is not the point. It is impossible to predict how history is going to utilize people's good intentions. Ethnologists and certain explorers were also just trying to understand different populations. It would be iniquitous to accuse the philosophers of the Enlightenment of harbouring sinister plans for the civilizations they made more accessible to the rest of the world and which thanks to them became better known and more respected. But that doesn't change the fact that what they did paved the way for the missionaries, merchants and colonial administrators. And now, at a time when idealistic thinkers want to see more peaceful relations between North and South, the multinationals are literally buying back the Developing World for a song through privatizations.

This little flashback doesn't only show that the old wounds still haven't healed. It also explains why the North and the South are not really listening to each other. Culture is not something abstract and the same holds for the relationships that could be built on it. The way Europeans imagine cultural exchange seems to have something to do with the belief in the end of History. Since they see others in their own image, they assume that identities overlap neatly with homogeneous nations which will either be happy or not so happy, but which will definitely have a sound legal framework. On this basis, any nation is therefore supposed to be able to say to another: here we all are now and the dark times are over. We each have our own memories, I have suffered a lot on the way here and so have you, no doubt. At last we can talk as true friends. The only problem is that the equality they postulate does not exist. If the subject wasn't so serious, such a misunderstanding would make you laugh, because it's so comical. In a place like Switzerland in December 1999, the hottest topic of conversation was 'the dignity of plants.' People declared that they are living beings and that we must not continue to maltreat them. Nobody has said so far that plants have a soul, but that can happen any minute. An ethics committee was appointed, in all seriousness, to make sure that in future this issue will be monitored on an ongoing basis. What commonalities are there really between this country and one from the Developing World where children are dying like flies from hunger and diseases? It is almost as implausible to think of these two different countries as actually being on the same planet, under the same sun and at the end of the day, we wonder whether maybe geography is playing tricks on us.

Despite the fact that the game is never entirely over, the West does not have much reason for concern. A certain author aptly compared it to a placid old man, sitting in his garden and enjoying the sunshine and the flowers.

He is blissfully oblivious of the fact that the impoverished inhabitants of this planet are in the process of killing each other deep down at the bottom of the chasm where slavery and colonization left them. The civil wars in Africa, Asia or Latin America seem to defy any sort of reason. The truth is that the origin of all of them, from the conflict in Kashmir to the crisis in the Great Lakes region, can easily be traced back to colonization. Unlike the West, these people are trying to recover their lost identity. Such are the ravages left behind by the European 19th century.

The main reason for all this trouble may also be the most straightforward one: those in contact with the West feel there is nothing left to discover. It is omnipresent. With its languages, its consumer goods and sometimes even its rituals, it is unsurpassed at opening the door to personal success. The favelas of Rio de Janeiro, just like the shanty towns of Yaoundé or Calcutta are bristling with thousands of satellite dishes turned towards the sky, like so many hands stretched out towards that 'somewhere else', the stuff of everybody's most cherished dreams. One gets to know about the cities and the way of life in these faraway places as well as their most famous artists and sports stars. They can tell all the television presenters from CNN and the European channels apart by their personal quirks. Who is still interested in hearing an artist from New York talk about his daily life? It may not be such a bad idea, since he could warn young Africans and Asians to be on their guard against certain clichés.

Paradoxically, it's these very clichés which form the essence of their American Dream and we have to face the fact that trying to deprive them of it means plunging them into despair. On the other hand, do we know so little about Africa that we can only mention this one example? For the West, Africa remains *terra incognita.* Here is an interesting anecdote: when a senator from Arkansas, after hearing that a genocide was going on in Rwanda, wanted to know a little bit more about that country, someone told him it was close to Zaïre. The senator, rather non-plussed, then asked, "But where is Zaïre?" Admittedly, the Western press is trying to reverse this trend. It is quite common for the more important daily papers to dispatch a reporter to some Southern part of the World, tasked with gathering information about the current political and social situation. The journalist is usually inured to the danger of misrepresentation he is exposed to and will take special care to do his work diligently. The trouble is that his freedom is often curbed by what the readers want to know about these Southern countries. Even if he thinks that they have not asked the right questions, he still has to come up with answers to them in a very short space of time. So he ends up with a very detailed report which is factually correct, but which has seemingly very little to do with reality. It is true that this kind of reporting is only aimed at putting across a simple snapshot of life without wanting to burden the reader with heavy in-depth analyses. That it is both relevant and legitimate is not in doubt. But it is worrying that this is practically the only available source of information about Africa. The average person from the North has no way of knowing how the Africans themselves conceive of their difficulties, nor is anyone helping him understand the new dynamic which is taking hold of this continent. In other words, the image the West has of the others is almost identical to its prejudices.

It is clear that the economic disparities will not go away in a hurry. They are the reason, in fact, why any attempt to bring the North and the South closer together, seems doomed to failure.

The wall of incomprehension is alive and well. To deny it would be unrealistic, but to accept it would be suicidal. The survival instinct inherent in our species demands that different sensibilities be brought into contact with each other. On both sides of the barrier, we find men and women who are not happy with the *status quo*. They know what caused the disasters and deadlocks they have to contend with today and they are ready to embark on a completely new path, despite being aware that it won't be easy.

That is the reason why the idea that change is built on exchange is probably a lot more prevalent than people think. The statutes of UNESCO, the famous international cultural organization, stipulate that, 'If wars are conceived in the human mind, the bulwarks of peace must be erected in the human mind as well'. Steinbeck says more or less the same thing when he sees armed conflict as 'proof that relationships between people are generally not governed by intelligence.' This conviction does not come out of the blue. In so many different ways, thinkers and artists from all around the world have always tried very hard to etch this into human consciousness. And we know now that any culture that turns its back on the others is a threat to the rest of humanity. We had to go through two World Wars, the nuclear apocalypse of Hiroshima, as well as several appalling genocides and bouts of ethnic cleansing before those who have had enough of listening to the language of hate finally got the chance to make themselves heard in a very modest way.

Judging by the more or less recent civil wars in Africa or the situation in Iraq, in the Lebanon or in Chechnya, the task before us is still huge. It may seem quite naïve to suggest that violence can be eliminated, roots and all. It is an enormous undertaking, which has to be tackled over and over again. And yet, so far, there is no better way to prevent the devastation of wars.

Much work is being done in this regard and while nobody expects any miracles, every little bit helps. Since we cannot turn the world inside out, it is better to do a little bit of good than none at all. It so often happens that an artist, full of big ideas, arrives in a foreign city, far from home. It was difficult for him to cross the border, but he made it and he has arrived, complete with his imagination and his vision of the world, which is unlike any other. He talks to strangers either about his work or the joys and the suffering of his compatriots. He is a free man. His stories are subtle and sometimes even a little bit crazy. He is a smuggler of emotions. They, too, have to cross a border. Just in their head, of course, but so what?

The centre pages of the daily papers regularly announce cultural events. We are invited to listen to a conference about Miles Davis in Osaka, to visit an exhibition about the Vikings in Caracas, to participate in a Japanese haiku competition in Amsterdam or to watch the Indian dancer Shantala Shivalingappa at the Théâtre des Abbesses in Paris. There is so much going on. The headlines can make you dizzy, yes, they are even moving. Reading them, one is sometimes reminded of the letters readers send to newspapers because they are psychologically distressed. They may be lonely. They are looking for people to write to in faraway places to give them a taste of this difference, which to them is like a forbidden fruit. And strangely enough, these frenetic exchanges between very different countries are tinged with a great fear of solitude. They are a bit like love letters between the nations. It is almost like a herd instinct that brings artists from all over the world together in a place that seems dangerous to them. One could imagine a picture by a naïve painter: two fragile little birds huddled up against each other in a tree while a storm is raging all around them, sweeping everything away.

That is why we shouldn't laugh when an Australian poet, sipping his drink at one of these evening cocktail parties remembers *dreamtime* and almost bursts into sobs while he is talking about the Golden Age of his people, the time before the arrival of the barbarian civilizers from the West. The pretentiousness of these social gatherings may be irritating and make you snigger, but one should probably see it as a chance for decent people to get to know each other. These gatherings are always very cosmopolitan and that is a good reason why they should continue to take place. One may ask oneself, of course, how someone from Copenhagen will feel about having the use of ivory hunting horns from ancient Tibet explained to him. How important can these ritual objects possibly be to a visitor who has just got off the train after yet another exhausting day in his life during which he has understood absolutely nothing? It is a nostalgic affair and it is quite possible that, in a shadowy sort of way, it has a lot to do with a previous existence. In every human being, the longing for what is far away, which also includes childhood, is easily re-awakened.

This silent inner dialogue, via the intermediary of another culture, is a precious moment which elicits many completely new associations. It certainly has nothing in common with the cheap thrills tourists seek in exotic destinations. The tourist often just takes a few reluctant steps outside his familiar surroundings in order to reassure himself of the superiority of his way of life and value system. He measures everything he sees by his own standards and one has the feeling that he has eyes at the back of his head and has only come to spoil everything. The exercise is legitimate, but he should not pretend that he is doing it all out of concern for the others, which is simply not true. Most tourists who decide to go to Kenya, go there because they want to see gorillas and not Kenyans. It is a great shame, but that is how it is. It is interesting that certain countries in the South have started promoting what they call 'cultural tourism', in order to give these organized trips a human dimension. Unfortunately, this laudable concept was immediately robbed of its potential meaning by the dictates of profitability. All that is left of it is a tribute of vice to virtue, but that is at least something. It is an undeniable fact that culture always forms the shortest path between two nations.

Novels and films are not only more accessible than learned sociological treatises, but they also allow us to gain far more in-depth knowledge about a human society. When a dramatist, over and above the performance of his work also gets the chance to address a foreign audience, he can communicate to them a more exact idea of what is going on in his country. This is how numerous creative artists, under persecution by dictators, have managed to attract the world's attention to human rights violations in their countries. Even if the artists simply tell the outside world what it is like to live in these densely populated towns and villages, it will help correct many prejudices. And besides, just describing the daily worries of the ordinary people can sometimes have a greater subversive power than grandiose ideological petitions. What matters is to keep the dialogue going: terror can only blossom in silence.

For these reasons, cultural exchange creates a platform for artists who can, very quickly, become the voice of those without a voice. Their words tend to have a great impact, because they are usually reported by the media. In certain cases – in Eastern Europe, in South Africa or in Latin America, – they have succeeded in putting an end to totalitarian regimes. The Nigerian Wole Soyinka, winner of the 1986 Nobel Prize for literature could not prevent the odious hanging of the author Ken Saro-Wiwa and his eight Ogoni companions, but he made a big contribution towards putting his country back on the road to democracy and normality.

The same kind of opportunity also arises out of the phenomenon of globalization, which so often elicits a sense of distaste. The existence of a public, international voice, conscious of its power, is quite new. It means that today, a painter or a writer has a better chance to become internationally known than even a few years ago. It is difficult to decide whether he should rejoice about this fact or regret it. For some people, the mass consumption of cultural products is always suspect. Others, by contrast, interpret it as a sign of democratization that had to come, for better or for worse.

Many countries, which have failed to allocate sufficient funds to cultural events, have allowed the multinationals to get involved. They have not hesitated to organize a sort of international fair of the soul, and they have taken possession of all the lucrative forms of artistic expression. The others, which were cynically considered as counter-productive, were left to the governments. The industrialists, who are not very interested in artistic subtlety, made every effort to homogenize individual taste at a global level. One of the consequences of this was that the national film industries have been strangled. In the era of super-productions, a talented director is not even really necessary anymore to guarantee the success of a movie. It is a film industry with tried and tested formulas based on the assumption that the spectators are all big children who need to be amazed.

And it is more or less the same with the so-called 'world music.' The only difference being that here, the various available ways of broadcasting mean that the musician has to find a compromise between dissimilar audiences. He himself is content to stay relatively close to his roots but also to make sure they do not get in his way. However, it certainly is not great art. It is simply a matter of keeping the film- or music industry going. If the comparison wasn't so unpleasant, one would be tempted to call them cultural products on steroids, reminiscent of the sad example of chickens and such like.

In Europe, certain circles have fathomed this danger. The reaction is often harsh criticism of America, since this is rightly perceived as the place where the whole problem started. This fight, which is led by respected intellectuals, has resulted in the European nations paying more attention to culture. But by and large, governments still don't pay it the attention it really deserves and politicians are finding it difficult to sympathize with artists who are labouring for posterity, while they can rarely see very far beyond the date of their next election.

Naturally, down South, the situation is worse. Overwhelmed as they are by seemingly insurmountable problems, the developing countries tend to consider culture as a luxury. They simply cannot afford to subsidize theatre companies or publishers. Even if the days when intellectuals were systematically thrown into prison are over, it will still take a while before they are actively encouraged to criticize the powers that be. Despite that, we can't get away with just saying that the South lacks the means to turn its cultural and educational plans into reality. It is much worse than that, since actually, countries in the South are *not even allowed* to allocate substantial resources to these areas. The few countries which have tried to do it, in a sort of desperate bet on the future, have seen the bosses from the North – the gentlemen of the World Bank, to be exact – frown upon their actions and threaten to kill them by slow strangulation.

It is embarrassing but true that unless the North is prepared to pay for these friendly exchanges between the nations, both on its own doorstep and further afield, nothing ever happens. That is also why the co-operation among the Southern countries is so poor as to be almost non-existent. Many of the artists from these countries are touring the big cities of the North and putting on their shows in all the most famous and prestigious venues, while hardly ever getting the chance to compare notes with other African or Asian performers. If such encounters do take place, either on African soil or, a lot more frequently in Europe, they are always financed by the latter. A book fair in Abidjan or a contemporary art exhibition in Dakar would be unthinkable without the financial backing of an organization like the European Union or one of the developed countries acting in isolation. Numerous writers or filmmakers from the South feel it is better for their career simply to move to London, Paris, New York or Geneva. This can lead to the paradoxical situation where a talented sculptor is highly esteemed abroad, but barely known at home. It is quite possible that, in the course of his career, he ends up losing all contact with the early sources of his inspiration.

From an artistic point of view, this can be very damaging indeed.

If either political censorship or logistical problems make it impossible for a director to show his movies in his own country, he will, often without even realizing it himself, start producing films for the only audience he has at his disposal. And this audience is obviously exclusively foreign. If he lacks moral fibre, this moviemaker is more focused on the panels of judges at the most popular European and American festivals than anything else and gives more credence to certain Western critics than to those from his own country. Basically, his one and only goal is to get a foot in the door where people can still afford a movie ticket. Certain European producers who make movies set in Africa have understood this only too well and since they also have a very good idea of the sort of scenario that will attract funding without necessarily having to make a profit, their films tend to be exotic to the point of buffoonery and loaded with ambiguous nods to the average European viewer. There is a more and more obvious tendency in African cinema to offer movies that are so blatantly superficial that they leave the true Africa connoisseur baffled. It can drive you mad to think that a continent has lost control over the kind of image it wants to convey to the rest of the world. This is a peculiar process which shows that poverty can lead to unexpected humiliations.

To think about the trend – the word also signifies *direction* – underlying this North-South exchange is a priority. The fact that these meetings usually take place in the North and are almost exclusively financed by the latter, ought to make its partners proud, or at least enlightened. This imbalance gives the North an immense power, making it the sole legitimizing force of the cultural actors of the South. We all know well that it lies in the nature of power to be exercised exclusively by him who holds it. The temptation is great to shift financial subsidies to those artists in the developing countries who are working in their original cultural sphere. Most people share this opinion, by the way. A few years ago, the French government made a gesture that seemed quite noble at first sight – it became easier for intellectuals and artists from francophone Africa to obtain a visa. The reason for this generosity quickly came to light. It was a case of stemming the tide of African academics being lost to American universities and thus to the English language. In the thinking of the francophone decision-makers, that was *shocking* and not really *politically correct.* The countries of the South are more or less openly expected to form an alliance against America which, it is true, seems to go to extraordinary lengths in trying to unite the entire universe against itself.

Nobody suffers as much from globalization as the countries of the South which have become even more marginalized as a result. But if these countries are engaged in the fight against the stultifying Americanization of the world, it must above all be in order to defend their interests that in certain major respects, are in conflict with those of Europe. Some of them are talking to us about cultural diversity by asking us to join their battle cry, 'Unite against Uncle Sam'! Things really cannot be so simple. There is a certain arrogance involved in wanting to turn francophone Africans into a supplementary force against America for example, on the basis of a language which is bringing them closer to their former colonizer but is separating them from the rest of Africa. This is certainly a significant problem and one has to find a solution for it. Our nations would definitely be in a better position if their leaders had, despite the lack of funds, enough insight to grasp the strategic significance of culture. In addition, what matters before we even start planning an encounter with others, is to make sure that we are 'putting our souls in a safe place.' This is the advice the novelist Cheikh Hamidou Kane gave us forty years ago. It has never been more up to date. One cannot expect morally completely pure intentions from any nation. In some way, cultural exchange should be left to the creators alone. They still have the strength to be naïve and are less Manichean. Through their contact with American artists, for example, they have learnt that their counterparts despise standardization as much as they do. Every creator worthy of the name will agree that quality is conditional upon individuality and that cultural creations must reflect the soul of the people and not what the market dictates. Mass production is an increasingly casual – and dangerous – way of making more and more profit, born as much out of contempt for people as for their culture.

Thanks to the ongoing debate about globalization, everybody must have noticed a kind of awe, bordering on fascination, for what is old and handcrafted. The battle between Roquefort and Burger King is a more recent manifestation of the eternal fight between Good and Evil. In fact, the issue here is not really food, but respect for the past.

That may be why cultural encounters are sometimes reminiscent of rituals for the dead: they celebrate objects which seem doomed to obsolescence, or rather, oblivion. But they nevertheless do have their place in that they are tributes to pure artistic value, acknowledgements of things that does not cost anything and have no practical use. As such, they counterbalance the aspect of globalization that reduces creativity to a vulgar *ersatz* in music and in literature, destroys people's identity and lowers their sensibilities to the lowest common denominator.

It is also possible that yet another danger is hidden here; nostalgia for the old days can make you forget that culture is the expression of a dynamic human reality. What about avant-garde art works which look towards the future?

There are artists still bold enough to go off the beaten track. They are known to just a few cognoscenti, but they deserve to be heard. With them, everything seems possible. They are so free that they seem to be slightly out of touch with reality. But apart from that, things are quite simple, they neither say they are from the North nor from the South. In the words of a certain philosopher, they are convinced that no one was there before them, which means they are free of prejudice. Their attraction for what is virginal, absent and void makes them genuine mutants.

But even with them, the game is not won as a matter of course, since nothing human is ever simple. The time has not yet come when a foreigner can go wherever he wants unnoticed. I will remember the booming, 'Buon giorno, signore!' which welcomed me when I walked through the door at the Ristorante della Posta at Carona, for a long time to come. It had Mediterranean warmth, which means it wasn't a fake. And yet, my arrival definitely caused a bit of a commotion, however discrete. And then word gets around. It is enough to be a dawn watcher, like Mandela on Robben Island. It is a question of patience and passion. At Carona, I ended up getting a slice of the true story about Charlie the Pig.

And Roberto is right, of course: things like that also happen in my country. All we had to do was to tell each other.

Negro-African Identity and Globalization

At the beginning of the 1990s, the young Burkinabé producer Idrissa Ouédraogo coined a phrase which has become famous. He said, "I am not an African filmmaker, I am just a filmmaker." After that, it became quite normal for the younger African novelists, painters and musicians wanting to escape the straitjacket of their negritude, to introduce themselves as citizens of the world. The fact that this coïncides with the end of the Cold War is surely not fortuitous. These declarations, coming from black African creative artists, have made a clean break with previous decades when intellectuals from this continent seemed to be largely concerned with rebuilding their damaged Black identity after centuries of slavery and colonization. Why is it that their heirs suddenly feel like spitting out their roots like a bitter fruit? It may be that the murder of their fathers resuscitated something like a survival instinct in them. Not only did the fall of the Berlin Wall signal the collapse of communism, it was also a strong hint that economically, the world was moving on from inter-nation trade to a global network. The young African producers were not keen to buck this trend and therefore refused to lock themselves into a debate which was considered obsolete and possibly born out of a sense of inferiority.

Above all, they wanted to move with the times. It seemed as though the demise of the ideologies – always postulated but never proven – was tantamount to the demise of thought itself, before globalization became almost overnight, the new universal standard, to the point where some people now see it as a 'new form of obscurantism.'

But this is not all bad. Artists from every continent even see it as a way of realizing their dream of a homogeneous and therefore peaceful humanity.

They are painting, making movies or writing, with others like themselves in mind, scattered in all four corners of the planet and that has added a fresh stimulus to contemporary artistic creation.

Culture has, in fact, become a fully-fledged industry like never before, making creative artists rich and allowing millions of others to earn a decent living.

But turning art into a commodity creates other problems which are a lot less positive. Faceless managers have usurped the place of the genuine artist, sacrificing the depth and uniqueness of artworks on the altar of profitability. In order to keep the emotion-mill turning, the public is encouraged to consume mass produced goods which have no lasting value but can be endlessly copied and multiplied.

Besides, this globalization sidelines the poorer individuals and nations to the extent that one might accuse it of being full of empty promises, or worse still, a betrayal. Despite the undeniable progress that has been made, access to information and know-how remains very uneven. On a planet where 20% of human beings share 85% of all available resources, 855 million people can neither read nor write and 820 million do not have enough to eat. It is absurd and actually insulting to lecture people about the benefits of the information highways before they even have access to electricity and clean drinking water!

If France, one of the rich countries, could clamour and demand to be treated as a 'cultural exception' in order to protect its movie industry, what can Mozambique, Madagascar or Nigeria do in the same situation? These three countries belong to a continent whose contribution to global export, according to the WTO, increased by 1% in 2004, versus 18.1% for Europe, 12.3% for the United States and 8.5% for Japan alone.

The battle against poverty is preventing these countries from dedicating the necessary funds to culture and the resulting vacuum is immediately filled by the multinationals. And this, in turn, is why African artists are tempted to sell their soul by trading their creations in the global market place.

In some cases this can of course work to their advantage. African music, for example, has managed to make a real profit out of this new situation. Because the technicalities of distribution are easy and due to its being folklore with a universal appeal, it is responsible for many impressive personal success stories. There is a heavy price to pay for this, though, since the worldwide popularity of certain musicians forces the others to follow their example by adapting the authentic African sound to the taste of a global, mostly Western audience. It is a sad fact that these great African musicians are only admired at home after they have first been successful abroad. Their strong presence in what Jean-Pierre Warnier calls the 'media catchment area'[97] is enough to guarantee them fame and fortune. Everybody knows the rules of the game and in this business where money is more important than art, not even the musician himself is entirely free of cynicism. He is well aware that with "world music" being such a hotchpotch nowadays, his target audience has to be the universal Mr. Average with a fondness for exoticism. One doesn't know whether one should be sad or happy about this: after all, the music industry provides jobs and dreams for thousands of young Africans and gives millions of them the feeling of being actively involved in a cutting-edge global phenomenon. The most attractive aspect of globalization is probably the ease with which the youth of the entire world communicate with each other in a musical language which is more or less inaccessible to adults.

The damage African cinema has suffered is much more serious. Soon after gaining independence, all the African countries made a big effort to develop their own movie-production policy, to produce films – against all the odds – and to ensure their distribution. Filmmakers like Sembène Ousmane, Mohammed Lakhdar-Hamina or Med Hondo tried to endow these movies, right down to their mutual differences, with a vision of the future for nations in the process of remaking themselves. It was, of course, not difficult for the Hollywood super-productions and also for French films, which are omnipresent on the small screen, to throw obstacles in their way.[98] Structural adjustment programmes, a term which stands for incisive funding cuts in the cultural sector, have profoundly upset cinematic production. In Senegal, between 1992 and 1999, 18 out of 38 movie theatres have disappeared. In Algeria, where only three films have been produced since 1995, the number of cinemas has shrivelled from 400 in 1986 to only about 20 in 2000.

Today, African cinema is almost completely controlled by foreign interests. France continues to finance movies in its former colonies through its Ministry of Co-operation. Private Canadian and French movie producers, too, are taking a controlling interest in this sector under the pretext of francophone co-operation.

This has completely changed both the aesthetic approach and the subject choices of the African film directors who currently get most of the media exposure. Their movies, conceived with Western film festivals in mind, are almost never watched in Yaounde or in Libreville.

They may bear African signatures, but they reflect a foreign perspective of the continent. One could almost call this a hostile takeover of ideas, since the director, having been progressively divested of his original scenario, ends up by contributing nothing but his name.

And only too often, the producer stipulates that the majority of 'his' camera crew must be made up of European or Canadian technicians.

This uncomfortable situation does not only affect African directors, but the issue here is more a cultural than a commercial one. Those who manage to keep a stranglehold over the images of a continent, can quite easily also become its political and social masterminds.

At first sight, the book industry does not give the impression of having successfully resisted globalization. Senegal for example, which together with Ivory Coast is one of the few francophone countries in Africa where the situation still has some economic viability, has for more than a decade had only two booksellers worthy of the name. The *Nouvelles Éditions Africaines du Sénégal* and the *Nouvelles Éditions Ivoriennes* have been bought back by Havas and Hachette.

However, we must not forget that globalization may have worsened the book crisis in Africa, without having caused it. Its impact on the textbook market has been less damaging than on literary books. Since the latter are in the so-called international languages, they would certainly have deserved a larger audience than the one they actually have. The Western readership, very reduced in numbers, will often read an African book more in order to discover new cultural territory rather than out of interest in the author. A Norwegian or an Italian wanting to learn about the continent might well prefer to approach African culture by way of its music, its theatre, its dance and film festivals than through its novels or poetry.

The fact that it is difficult for an African author to break into the world market is not necessarily a bad thing. In the knowledge that he cannot live by his pen, he can take every aesthetic liberty and imbue his writing with his true convictions for all time to come. On the other hand, one should not simply put up with a situation which represents a step in the wrong direction. It is extremely illuminating to see how much the book crisis has weakened the circulation of ideas in Africa. That we no longer hear great African voices as in the days of the magazine *Présence Africaine*, is very significant. Soyinka's Nobel Prize in 1986 seems to have signalled the end of an era. The African book market used to be so much more extensive at the time when the names of Mongo Beti, Amos Tutuola, Mario de Andrade and Langston Hughes were all featured in one and the same anthology. Texts got translated very quickly and Léopold Sédar Senghor, Chinua Achebe and Richard Wright were famous names all over Africa. Today, francophone intellectuals know next to nothing about people like Pepetela, Chenjerai Hove or Ayi Kwei Armah and it would be pointless to think of what Patrick Chamoiseau, Gloria Naylor and Tanella Boni have in common.

By doing away with the sense of solidarity based on skin colour and a painful past, globalization has torn apart the African author's audience. It has shrunk a reservoir of readers that had already been severely eroded by a general decline in purchasing power. In trying to attract foreigners, the only audience still able to afford books, more novels are published in Africa than poetry. In 1998, Ahmadou Kourouma, winner of the Prix Renaudot in 2000, said regarding his book *Waiting for the Wild Beasts to Vote*: "I wrote this book primarily with the European reader in mind. I repeatedly explain the thinking behind magic, which is so profoundly different from the logic of the European." This sort of attitude has caused a large number of African authors to move to London, New York or Paris. While some of them were trying to get away from brutal regimes, others have simply chosen to be close to their actual readership. These authors, who no longer really know the Africa they are talking about, are unfortunately the only ones the rest of the world wants to listen to and who, as a result, we also listen to… in Africa. It is amazing that the great African authors who are alive today, whose works are recognized classics which are read and commented upon in schools, no longer have a media presence, especially in the francophone countries. They continue writing nonetheless, in the knowledge that their work does not match the Africa image which the all powerful Western literary establishment wishes to project nowadays. What they are doing 'wrong' is having too much strength of character to stick to the pre-selected topics which happen to be popular.

The impact of African literature largely depends on its linguistic background and the ulterior motives of the former colonial powers. France, unlike Britain, remains obsessed with the idea of having to defend its language and considers every francophone author as an accomplice in its battle against …the globalization of the English language. Authors writing in English do not have to fight this rear guard action; their working language comes as a package that includes a vast potential readership and all the rights and privileges of being effortlessly cosmopolitan. And yet, even they cannot hope to conquer the whole world simply by straddling one continent.

Be it cinema, literature or music, the best way of responding to globalization is to mount a counter-attack against it by building an African market. And although that has to be mostly the task of private stakeholders in each respective country, the political will has to be there too. Poverty and ignorance have a habit of feeding each other and creating a vicious circle, but those who perceive the cultural dimension of development correctly, will be the first to find a way out of it.

In fact, new strategies have already been tested. Sembène Ousmane formed a partnership with an oil company in order to finance his film *Faat Kiné* and other producers are trying to raise funds in South Africa or Nigeria.

In 1998, *Les Nouvelles Éditions Ivoriennes d'Abidjan* launched a collection entitled 'Adoras.' It is modelled on Western romance literature and features titles by Ivorian authors who write under a pseudonym. These short, sentimental stories are modestly priced and have been really successful. Some of them have been adapted for television by the French International Channel. The increased sales figures of the famous Onitsha and Kinshasa market literature are also due to globalization. In Nigeria, these novels are published in Yoruba and Hausa and are thus exclusively aimed at a local readership. In Dakar, thanks to the 'bargain-basement bookshops', one can buy the whole of Shakespeare for absolute giveaway prices.

All this shows that globalization needs to be constantly re-interpreted. Societies that have seemingly been sidelined by it, are always finding new ways of expressing themselves and surviving without necessarily yielding to its demands. Real culture is the response of the human spirit to the blindness of dictatorships, be they political or economic. It is never loud or flashy and it matures slowly, in deep and secret places. It is not by denying who they are, but by 'persevering in their being' (Cheikh Hamidou Kane), that creative artists will be able to face the challenges of an ever more complex and unforgiving world. An artist is nothing and has nothing to say unless he has learnt to be himself first.

Invisible Cities and the Armchair Traveller

In it's heyday, millions of young people all over the world were mad about *The Little Red Book.* The extraordinary popularity of Maoism, quite difficult to explain nowadays, naturally made communist China's neighbour jealous. That is also the reason why, towards the end of the 1970s, the North Korean regime finally decided to let every nation on earth know that Kim Il-Sung, 'beloved leader of the Korean people' was far more infallible than Mao Tse Tung. After all, the latter only held the rather modest title of Great Helmsman…

So it happened that I found myself in Pyongyang, together with a bearded professor of philosophy by the name of Daniel D… who at the time was an executive member of the French communist party. We were there in order to revise the French translations of the work of the Peerless Commander.

Our hosts had gone to enormous trouble in trying to persuade us that we had come to the best place on earth. This was my one and only chance, but I am afraid that I simply didn't know how to seize it. I was neither interested in the model workers nor in the tree which Kim Il-Sung, clearly chosen by Fate, is supposed to have climbed at the age of five in order to catch the rainbow. It certainly seemed strange, seeing old women dressed in blue, sweeping a perfectly clean embankment each time a car had passed, which was about every thirty minutes, but it didn't impress me. I would gladly have exchanged all the staggering propositions of Djoutche[99] for the smile of a stranger. I didn't manage, I think, to talk to more than about three people in North Korea. I could try as I liked, but I could never get even one word out of our driver, a gentleman with an inscrutable face that was made even more impenetrable by his thick dark glasses. If he was ever kind enough to give a vague nod in our direction, I don't remember it. But it wasn't just him; some young person tiptoed into our house in our absence in order to clean up. Clearly, she had strict orders never to be there at the same time as the two foreigners. I was sneaky enough to succeed in catching a fleeting glimpse of her silhouette one day.

But all that pales into insignificance compared to the Wang affair, named after one of our two translators.

I will probably never know what has become of this stocky young man who was always in a white shirt, had a sparkle in his eye and spoke chaotic French. All I can say, twenty years after the event, is that Wang disappeared the day after he had taken it upon himself to let us get a little too close to the gymnasts in a stadium in order to admire their routine of synchronized movements. The thousands of adolescents we had surprised in the middle of their training were not supposed to cross our path even once in their lifetime. Most of them had probably never seen a black person, even on television. They were completely baffled and this little detour cost the unlucky Wang his freedom, or maybe even his life. At any rate, we never saw him again.

My strongest memory after one season in Pyongyang is all the things I didn't see there. North Korea is not the sort of country where one can ask just anybody questions and its capital struck me as so unreal, so desperately cut off from time and space, that I sometimes wonder whether I really ever set foot there. When I think back, it strikes me as a vast theatre stage full of silent, terrified shadows, trying to slip away and make themselves invisible.

However, the feeling of being trapped in an obscure and suffocating space is not uniquely associated with totalitarian societies. I sensed it again, very strongly, in the canton Aargau, a pleasant and prosperous part of German-speaking Switzerland. The night I arrived, I noticed some lights about a hundred metres away from where I had settled down in order to write *The Horseman and his Shadow* [Le cavalier et son ombre]. I had been told that that was the pulsating heart of Boswil, a hamlet of about three thousand people. It seemed quite natural to me to try and find out more about the village where I was going to be living for the next six months. So I spent two or three weeks exploring every nook and cranny of Boswil, but I hardly ever saw a soul. And meeting the odd cyclist or peasant who squints at you suspiciously is simply not enough of a distraction from the monotony of cold and deserted little country streets. I, the stranger, may not have had much chance to observe the locals, but I frequently felt watched from behind closed shutters. When finally Max and Francine Krummenacher came to see me from Zurich, I asked them sarcastically, "So where is it then, this village?" These two friends, who had visited Senegal, understood immediately what I meant. Wherever you happen to be in Dakar and you come across a group of about a dozen people, they'll make a hell of a noise. In Boswil, I found it hard to understand how as many as three thousand people could try so hard not to exist in a quasi-fictitious village.

It does happen, of course, that a city presents a thoroughly attractive picture to the newly arrived visitor. If I have loved Fez, then in the Lebanon, I have really only been fascinated by Baalbek and the Phoenician city which was excavated by masons right next to the harbour of Beirut. These thousand-year old ruins spoke to me much more than the nearly identical streets of Montreal or Berlin.

Since I was not able to truly experience these distant cities, I had to dream them after my return home. To dream is to tell others. Turning their wide-open eyes into the mirror where you can see what you had barely glimpsed before. The moment I step outside Dakar airport, the sweat may be making my skin sticky and a gust of hot wind is lashing my face, but the story is just waiting for the first opportunity to unfold its wondrous fabrications. I know my family and friends can't wait to be thrilled by my wild adventures in exotic lands. I will not hesitate to embellish my tale. Either you are a novelist or you are not. And then, it is simply petty not to lie to your friends who are so eager to be amazed...

Alas, reality is not quite so simple. In this novel, the narrator is not who you think he is. It is rather me who should listen to others. The Senegalese think their country is the most beautiful in the world and I very quickly have the feeling they resent me for having been away for so long. With all the spectacular events I have missed, I must have many blanks in my head and Ndiack, my alter ego, or someone else, is trying to fill me in. Divorces, weddings, deaths, nothing is left out. I am told that such and such a politician has sold out again and that obscure quarrels have kept the country on tenterhooks for weeks. And the wedding of the president's son, you must have at least heard about it over there? Outrageous! For the wedding banquet, they flew in 30 chefs from Paris. By private plane, no less! My eyes are blazing with fury and I hear myself muttering, "The Bastards!" I have to admit, I love it, I love hearing about the little troubles of these wretched lives of ours. And yes, my indignation proves that I am really back in Senegal, the place where my heart belongs. If I was in Chicoutimi or in Moscow, what is going on there really has nothing to do with me.

After a week, the crowd downtown suddenly gives me a jolt. In Europe or in America, pedestrians walk along in an orderly manner in order to get to a specific place. In Dakar, Ndjamena or Abidjan – that's also home for me, the Chad and Ivory Coast – I always had the impression that panic reigns. People are running in all directions, you hear screaming from everywhere and in this mad circus, you might well bump into the same strange frenetic facial expressions in different places. The transition from the soft, straight lines of the rich world to this whirling chaos is almost a journey of its own. Coming from the sort of countries where people are content and know where they are going, one looks at one's own with different eyes. Here, you cannot relax because you never know what the next day will bring and you are going round and round in circles, covered in smoke and dust.

But it doesn't matter. As time goes by, I remember myself, as it were. Funny country, though, where nothing is quite as it should be. The streets are dirty, the politicians are a gang of corrupt weirdos and the poverty is humiliating. And yet, it is here where I feel most at ease. It is the only place on earth where I don't always have to check that I am myself, for fear of having turned into someone other. It is only here that I can make plans for the future, however uncertain that may be. But to realize all this, I have occasionally had to lose myself at the other end of the planet…

Africa Beyond the Mirror

Postscript

For better or for worse, the dates of significant political events become history and are forever cast in stone, while names and borders of countries may change overnight as a result of these very events.

The Rwandan Genocide of the Tutsis took place in 1994, and the original French edition of 'Africa beyond the Mirror' (*L'Afrique au-delà du miroir* by Éditions Philippe Rey: Paris) came out more than a decade later, in 2007. It is thanks to Ayebia Clarke Publishing Limited – an independent specialist African publisher committed to championing writing from Africa to an international readership – that this important, long-awaited book has now been made available in English.

Despite the long delay, the publishers and the writer have taken a joint decision not to change dates or other details in the text to preserve its authenticity.

At the same time, readers should be aware that 'Zaïre' officially became the 'Democratic Republic of Congo' in May 1997 and that the author, to be historically correct, intentionally uses the old name when talking about the notorious Mobutu era.

Regarding the potentially emotive terms 'negro' and 'negrophobia', we would like to point out that in 2005, the author co-wrote a book with Odile Tobner and the late François-Xavier Verschave in French, entitled *Négrophobie*. In many respects, 'Africa beyond the Mirror' can and should be regarded as a sequel to that earlier work. The connotations of the word 'negro' in a *francophone* context have always been somewhat more neutral than in the Anglo-Saxon world and especially in North America, but we nevertheless decided not to resort to a much broader alternative like 'Afrophobia' when translating 'négrophobie' into English.

Several chapter headings in this book are subtle allusions to titles of works by other well-known African authors. This equally applies to the name of the project *Écrire par devoir de mémoire*, which plays such a central role here: it harks back to Yambo Ouloguem's ground-breaking novel *Le devoir de violence.*

After giving much thought to how *Écrire par devoir de mémoire* might best be rendered in English, we eventually agreed on 'Writing against Oblivion', since all the more literal variations sounded too much like a clumsy trans–-lation to our ears.

Last but not least, we capitulated in the face of the contemporary current which clamours for ever more political correctness. Having relinquished the concise but equivocal term 'Black Africa' in favour of 'Sub-Saharan Africa', which has the advantage of being free of colour references but trips less lightly off the tongue, it has now been suggested we should substitute the latter with 'Africa South of the Sahara': a veritable mouthful, unwieldy and almost a sentence in its own right. At the end of the day, the countries in question may best be described through the tautology 'African Africa', since one is simply trying to distinguish them from the Maghreb region, which culturally and – dare we say it? – racially, has long been more Arabic than African. If the Arabs then object, insisting that they, too, are African – which of course they are – the issue will remain a linguistic and socio-anthropological conundrum.

But these are just conventions and formalities. Looking beyond the mirror, on the other hand, is uncomfortable and painful – Boubacar Boris Diop must be counted as one of a handful of voices today that force us to do so: they write and **refuse** to keep quiet, and it is no doubt largely due to their courage if negrophobia in its basest forms is less of an issue today than it used to be.

Vera Wülfing-Leckie (primary translator)
Caroline Beschea-Fache (secondary translator)
17/01/2014

Notes

1 This masterpiece written about the last genocide of the twentieth century, that of the Tutsis in Rwanda, in 1994, has been translated from the French by Fiona Mac Laughlin, Bloomington, Indiana University Press, 2006.

2 Published in a book of interviews by Éloïse Brezault, *Afrique Paroles d'écrivains*, Paris, Mémoire d'encrier, 2010. B.B. Diop's interview is pp. 65 to 112. This passage that I translated from the French is on p. 69.

3 See the *Postcript* that B.B. Diop has recently written for a new edition of the French version of the novel: *Murambi, le livre des ossements*, Paris, Zulma, 2011; p. 246

4 Although nobody seems to know how it was calculated, this number seems to have been widely accepted by international organisations and the media. Such caution is partly due to the perfectly normal wish not to rely exclusively on the figures issued by the Rwandan government. Nevertheless, one senses a certain desire to minimise the extent of the genocide. And yet, even the lowest estimate, which clearly does not reflect the truth, remains terrifying: half a million victims in the short time-span of a hundred days!

5 Particularly the Interahamwe militias ('Those who are marching together').

6 Fest' Africa is an African literary festival in Lille, started by Ma mouna Coulibaly from Ivory Coast and Nocky Djedanoum from Chad, two journalists who came to France to study and have been living there ever since. It is organised by the *Association Arts et Métiers d'Afrique.*

7 This is a list of the names as well as the titles of *the texts published by each of the writers in this group: Monique Ilboudo (*Burkina Faso), *Murekatete, Le Figuier*/Fest'Africa, 2000; Véronique Tadjo (*Côte d'Ivoire), L'Ombre d'Imana,* Actes Sud, 2000,*[The Shadow of Imana, Journey to the Edge of Rwanda];* Koulsy Lamko (Chad), *La Phalène des collines,* Le Serpent à Plumes, 2002, *[The Butterfly of the Hills];* Nocky Djedanoum (Chad), *Nyamirambo, Le Figuier*/Fest'Africa, 2000; Meja Mwangi (Kenya), *Great Sadness, unpublished;* Abdourahman Waberi (Djibouti), *Moisson des crânes,* Le Serpent à Plumes, 2000, *[Harvest of the Skulls];* Tierno Monenmbo(Guinea*),* L'Aîné des orphelins, Le Seuil, 2000, *[The Eldest of the Orphans];* Jean-Marie Vianney Rurangwa (Rwanda), *Le Génocide des Tutsi expliqué à un étranger, Le Figuier*/Fest'Africa, 2001, *[The Genocide of the Tutsis explained to a Foreigner];* Vénuste Kayimahe (Rwanda), *France-Rwanda: les coulisses du génocide. Témoignage d'un rescapé, L'Esprit frappeur*/Dagorno, 2003, *[Behind the Scenes of the*

Genocide]; Boubacar Boris Diop (Senegal), *Murambi, le livre des ossements,* Stock, 2000, *[Murambi: The Book of Bones].*

8 An association of survivors that also exists outside Rwanda; the name means 'Remember!'

9 *Fagaala* is an intentional distortion of the Wolof word *fagaagal,* meaning 'extermination.'

10 Stock, 1997

11 'quand la mémoire va ramasser du bois mort, elle rapporte le fagot qui lui plaît.'

12 Koulsy Lamko, for example, felt that it made no sense whatsoever to write a novel and then resume the same life as before, as though nothing had happened. So he stayed on in Rwanda for four years, from 1998 until 2002. During that time, he founded the Arts Centre at the university of Butare, while at the same time teaching literature and drama at the national university.

13 This text originally formed the preface to the book by the Rwandan Genocide survivor Yolande Mukagasana, *The Wounds of Silence* (Actes Sud, 2001), [Les Blessures du silence]. The French editor refused to go ahead with the publication on the grounds that François Mitterand had been implicated.

14 Yolande Mukagasana, *La Mort ne veut pas de moi,* Fixot, 1997.

15 Yolande Mukagasana, *N'aie pas peur de savoir,* Robert Laffont, 1999; J'ai lu, 2000.

16 Philip Gourevitch, *We have the pleasure to inform you that tomorrow, we will be killed with our families.* [Nous avons le plaisir de vous informer que, demain, nous serons tués avec nos familles], Denoël, 1999.

17 Nicolas Bancel, *"The French media faced with Rwanda.(About the involvement of France from 1990 until the genocide)",* ["Les Médias français face au Rwanda. (De l'intervention française de 1990 au génocide"), *Africultures* n° 30, January 2002. An irreplaceable analysis…

18 Bernard Debré, *The Return of the Mwami, The True Story of the Rwandan Genocides,* [Le Retour du Mwami, la vraie histoire des génocides Rwandais], Ramsay, 1998.

19 Mehdi Ba, *Rwanda: A French Genocide.* [Un génocide français], L'Esprit frappeur, 2000.

20 Jean-Pierre Chrétien, *The Genocide and the Media,* [*Les médias du génocide*], Karthala, éd. revue et augmentée, 2000.

21 Gérard Prunier, *Rwanda: The Genocide,* [Rwanda: Le génocide], Dagorno, 1998.

22 François-Xavier Verschave, *Genocidal Complicity? French Foreign Policy in Rwanda.* [Complicité de génocide? La politique de la France au Rwanda], La Découverte, 1994.

23 Patrick de Saint-Exupéry, *A Disgrace: France in Rwanda,* [L'Inavouable: la France au Rwanda], Les Arènes, 2004.

24 Colette Braeckmann, *The New Predators,* [Les Nouveaux Prédateurs], Fayard, 2003.

25 *Death, Despair, Defiance,* London, African Rights, 1994.

26 Coordinated by Alison des Forges for the International League of Human Rights and Human Rights Watch: *No Witness Must Survive,* Paris, Karthala, 1999.

27 Benjamin Sehene is the author of an essay entitled *The Ethnic Trap,* [Le Piège ethnique], Dagorno, 1999, and has also published, in 2005, a remarkable novel, at L'Esprit frappeur: *Fire Uunder the Cassock,* [Le Feu sous la soutane]. In this book, Sehene describes, from inside as it were and with an impressive refinement and realism, the changing emotions of a notorious priest-turned-genocidaire, who currently lives as a refugee in France.

28 After *The Genocide of the Tutsi Explained to a Foreigner,* [Le Génocide des Tutsi expliqué à un étranger], Le Figuier /Fest'Africa, 2000, in the context of the project "Rwanda: Writing against Oblivion", and then *A Rwandan on the Roads of Exile,* [Un Rwandais sur les routes de l'exil], L'Harmattan, 2005, Jean-Marie Vianney Rurangwa has just finished another novel due to be published by Harmattan, *At the Gate of Hell,* [Au sortir de l'enfer].

29 This situation started to change quite drastically in 2004, the 10th anniversary of the genocide. Among the works published since then are: Esther Muyawayo and Souâd Belhaddad, *Women Who Survived,* [Survivantes], Éditions de l'Aube, 2004 and *The Flower of Stephanie, Rwanda between Reconciliation and Denial,* [La Fleur de Stéphanie, le Rwanda entre réconciliation et déni], Flammarion, 2006; Révérien Rurangwa, *Genocided,* [Génocidé], Presses de la Renaissance, 2006; Annick Kayitesi, *We are still here,* [Nous existons encore], Michel Lafon, 2004 (preface by André Glucksmann); Chantal Umutesi, *Peace for the Soul,* [La paix dans l'âme], Klanba Éditions, 2004 (preface by Kwamé Ngoran); Madeleine Mukamuganga, *Rwanda, from Happiness to Horror. I was there.* [Rwanda, du bonheur à l'horreur. J'y étais.] Cultures croisées, 2005. One will notice the dominance of women in these literary testimonies.

30 Jean-Paul Gouteux, *The Dark Night of Rwanda: France's Involvement in the Century's Last Genocide,* [La Nuit rwandaise], Dagorno, 2001; *La Nuit rwandaise: l'implication française dans le dernier génocide du siècle,* édition augmentée, 2004.

31 This term goes back to the manner in which justice was served in Rwanda before the colonial conquest. On top of the hill, men with a reputation for integrity and experience acted as judges. The culprit was asked to pay a symbolic compensation in kind to the other party, which also accepted his apologies. The idea to revisit this ancient form of jurisdiction was inspired by practical considerations: it would have taken centuries to wade through the files presented before the tribunals, especially in a country where almost all the attorneys and magistrates had been assassinated. The need to learn to live together again meant that one had to move fast. Seeking to establish a diligent kind of jurisdiction without losing too much detail, the *gacaca* quickly appeared to be the ideal solution. Besides that, it basically allows us to leave the past behind and to embark on a sincere verbal exchange that is validated by the group. That makes it easier to get to a reconciliation which the victims do not perceive as imposed by a higher authority.

32 Jean-Paul Gouteux, *The Dark Night of Rwanda. The Implication of France in the Last Genocide of the Century,* [La Nuit rwandaise. L'implication française dans le dernier génocide du siècle], expanded edition, Dagorno, 2004.

33 Mitterrand knew exactly what he was saying and it was not by accident that he used the words "African chiefs" and "machete" side by side. He expects the images suggested by this to speak for themselves... This was the way he expressed himself in the presence of several ..."chiefs" of African states. It should be pointed out in passing that that shows how little respect he had for his underlings in his political backyard.

34 A parliamentary information committee presided over by the socialist deputy Paul Quilès, one of Mitterrand's acolytes. Tasked with investigating the role of France during the Rwandan Genocide, their report was submitted in December 1998 to the President of the National Assembly.

35 Apart from the Quilès Commission which has been mentioned before, the Belgian Senate set up a Parliamentary Commission of Inquiry into the events in Rwanda, which sat from April to December 1997; the commission of independent enquiry into the activities of the UN during the Rwandan Genocide in 1994, which was set up at the request of the UN Security Council. It was presided over by Ingvar Carlsson, a former Swedish Prime Minister, and one of the members was South-Korean and another Nigerian; then there was the report of Alison des Forges (under the direction of), *Leave None to Tell the Story,* [Aucun Témoin ne doit survivre], Karthala, 1999, an enquiry by Human Rights Watch and by the International Human Rights Federation; by Laure Coret and François-Xavier Verschave (dir.), *The Horror Which Hits Us in the Face. The French Government and the*

Genocide in Rwanda, [L'Horreur qui nous prend au visage.] L'État français et le génocide au Rwanda, Karthala, 2005: a report on the work done by the Citizens' Commission of Inquiry established by several Civil Society associations for the purpose of investigating the role of their respective countries; by the commission of enquiry of the Organisation of African Unity, 2000, which will be discussed at a later stage.

36 The investigators of the OAU also frequently express their disgust at the power games of *Françafrique,* so utterly mad in some respects...

37 The Canadian General Roméo Dallaire, who was in charge of the Minuar (United Nations Mission for the Assistance of Rwanda) during the genocide, wrote the following about this issue: "Several times in this book I have asked the question: *Are we all human beings or are some of us more human than the others?* Those of us who live in the developed countries behave as though our lives were worth more than the lives of the other people on this planet. An American army officer told me quite unashamedly that the lives of eight hundred thousand Rwandans weren't worth risking the lives of more than six American soldiers; after having lost six soldiers, the Belgians declared that the lives of the Rwandans did not justify risking the life of even one more Belgian soldier...", Roméo Dallaire, *I Shook Hands With the Devil,* [J'ai serré la main du Diable], Outremont, Éditions Libre Expression, 2003.

38 The investigators of the OAU also frequently express their disgust at the power games of *Françafrique,* so utterly mad in some respects...

39 "Those who march together". See p. 18.

40 *Rwanda: The Avoidable Genocide,* OAU report.

41 Rwandan Patriotic Front

42 Gérard Prunier, *Rwanda: History of a Genocide,* [Rwanda, Histoire d'un genocide], Dagorno, 1977. Prunier's views are all the more interesting since, in his capacity as a member of the department of international relations of the French Socialist Party, this professional historian was very closely involved with the deployment of Turquoise. He describes in detail and as an insider, how this operation was set up.

43 *The Horror Which Grips Us in the Face. The French State and the Rwandan Genocide, op.cit.*

44 Jean-Paul Gouteux, *The Dark Night of Rwanda...*op. cit.

45 Quoted in Jean-Paul Gouteux, *The Dark Night of Rwan*da..., op.cit.

46 From our perspective, the Africa policy of France ignores the left-right divide.

47 Jean-Philippe Rémy "The Errors and the Strange Witnesses of Judge Bruguière", *Le Monde,* November 28, 2006.

48 Christophe Ayad, "A Rwandan Witness Challenges Judge Bruguière," *Libération,* December 4, 2006. The article comprises a great deal of other pieces of equally insane information. One frequently can't help laughing, even though the issue is extremely serious.

49 Olivier Guland, *Le Pen, Mégret and the Jews,* [Le Pen, Mégret and the Jews], La Découverte, 2000.

50 Patrick de Saint Exupéry, *The Disgrace: France in Rwanda,* [L'Inavouable, la France au Rwanda], op. cit.

51 He was Minister of Foreign Affairs in the coalition government during the genocide.

52 Patrick de Saint Exupéry, *The Disgrace: France in Rwanda,* [L'Inavouable, la France au Rwanda], *op. cit.*

53 Here it is difficult to decide whether the former minister expresses himself in this manner due to embarrassment or out of bad faith. The "international community" had already pronounced its "mea culpa" at the time when these conversations were recorded by RFI. M. Juppé could not ignore the fact that in 2004 – in addition to Belgium – the United

States, the OUA and the UN had publicly presented their excuses to the Rwandan people.

54 They are: *Aircrige* (Association internationale de recherches sur les crimes contre l'humanité): The International Association for Research on Crimes against Humanity), *Cimade* (Service oecuménique d'entraide): Oecumenical Service for Mutual Assistance, *Obsarm* (Observatoire des transferts d'armement): Arms Trafficking Watch, and *Survie.*

55 This observation is not intended to deny non-Africans the right to comment on our problems, nor does, for obvious reasons, this remark concern the authors from the Great Lakes region. And African fiction which has appeared in the wake of the project 'Rwanda: Writing Against Oblivion'– has earned the genocide an increasingly prominent position.

56 South Africa is an exception. The fight against Apartheid has demonstrated that the mobilization of the whole continent is both necessary and desirable.

57 WADR is a regional branch of the Open Society Initiative for West Africa (Osiwa). It has "offices [...] in each one of the three member countries of the River Mano Union, which are Guinea, Liberia and Sierra Leone." It is significant that this project, as well as some others in the broadcasting sector, is seeing the light of day now. This shows that the end of the foreign media monopoly in Africa is probably irreversible even if it is perhaps not quite round the corner.

58 Cheikh Anta Diop, *Nations nègres et culture*, Présence Africaine, 1954.

59 Cf. Cheikh M'Backé Diop: Cheikh Anta Diop, the Man and his Work, [Cheikh Anta Diop, l'homme et l'œuvre], Présence Africaine, 2003, p.54. The author, trained as a scientist himself, is the oldest son of the scholar. This could have brought about a book that was nothing but a hagiography. But this is not the case, on the contrary, he refuses any sort of vitriol, while nevertheless spelling out some uncomfortable truths. The result is a sober biography with a great sense of propriety, which above all takes care to publish only proven and verifiable facts. It succeeds brilliantly in shedding light on the ideas as well as the life of Anta Diop.

60 Cheikh Anta Diop, «The Art of Disguise» [L'art de contrefaçon], Taxaw, Dakar, March 1979.

61 The same holds for Gaston Berger and Daniel Sorano. The second university of Senegal and the Grand National Theatre in Dakar were named after them. Who were Gaston Berger and Daniel Sorano? The large majority of our compatriots know absolutely nothing about them, even if they had some kind of vague connection with our country. Maybe they even deserved the honour bestowed on them by Senghor. The only problem is that he took this decision solely based on what he, and he alone, thought of these two men. The result is that they are part of our collective memory in a purely abstract fashion.

62 This point deserves special attention. Everybody who questions the imperialist designs of Francophonie gets the same answer: "You don't understand, this great idea was born in Africa because of three great African leaders who were great lovers of the French language!" One might even be told that these leaders put France under pressure. And that the latter, which today is having to spend colossal sums in order to keep Francophonie going, gets absolutely nothing out of it. This is of course not the way it really is...

63 There is the well-known anecdote about General de Gaulle who, irritated by Bokassa's manners, said to him: "Stop calling me Papa, Mr. President." Bokassa's reply was, "Yes, Papa!" He may have had some serious Oedipal issues, but Bokassa was the Head of an "independent" State with voting rights in the UN. Only the most mischievous people would surmise that he went along with the decisions of his "Papa" at all times.

64 Nelson Mandela, *A Long Walk To Freedom,* [Un long Chemin vers la liberté], Fayard; LGF, Le Livre de Poche, 1996.

65 Nelson Mandela, *A Long Walk To Freedom*, Little Brown & Co., 1995.

66 *Le Monde*, January 5, 2002. It should also be noted that the *Canard Enchaîné* offered a rather original explanation for this indifference on the part of the French authorities. In essence, it said: it's Senghor's own fault, why did he have to die during the Christmas holidays; couldn't he have chosen a more convenient time?

67 This qualification, which is based on an extremely competitive exam or *concours*, entitles the holder to teach at the highest level in secondary and tertiary education. In most subjects, the number of candidates exceeds the number of places available. The successful *agrégé/-ée* is then committed to five years of service in either a state school or a university. (Cf: Oxford Dictionary)

68 White people in Wolof.

69 "Conversation with Bara Diouf" [Entretien avec Bara Diouf], *La Vie Africaine* no 6, March–April 1960. Quotation by Cheikh M'Backé Diop, *Cheikh Anta Diop, The Man and His Work*, ["L'homme et son oeuvre"] op. cit., p. 28.

70 "Interview with Bara Diouf", *La Vie africaine*, op. cit.

71 Aimé Césaire, *Discourse on Colonialism, translated by Joan Pinkham, Monthly Review Press, New York, 1972, p.35.*

72 Cheikh M'Backé Diop, *Cheikh Anta Diop, The Man and his Work, op. cit.*

73 To comply with the law, the party changed the name of the newspaper. The name *Siggi* ('to get back up', in Wolof), was changed to *Taxaw* ('to remain standing'). Sembène Ousmane, who also had a serious political bone to pick with Senghor, was in the same situation. According to Senghor, there was one *d* too many in the title of the film *Ceddo*, which he directed in 1977, but neither the director–cum- author, nor the country's most eminent linguists thought he was correct. The frenzied linguistico-ideological fall-out of this affair can only make us smile today. Sembène refused to yield, but the President used his political power to ban the film for seven years in Senegal, until its "premiere" at the National Daniel Sorano Theatre in Dakar on July 4, 1984.

74 "What these people are saying in French in their National Assembly over there, oh well, if I was to translate it into Wolof for you, you would only want to do one thing and that is to beat them up!" He has never named any names, but it is a safe bet that apart from the deputies, he was referring to Senghor, who liked to adorn his speeches with learned Greek and Latin phrases and quotations from Gide or Goethe.

75 "One has told our people so many lies that it has become dangerous to tell them the simple truth, since that might plunge them into despair!"

76 This comment is not aimed at Senghor, who was definitely above such shallow demagoguery. We have already seen that he, the native of Joal, was both absolutely himself and at the same time another.

77 One should note in passing that this was Cheikh Anta Diop's only stay in the US. This is extremely surprising considering the enormous impact his thinking had in the Americas and particularly in large segments of the Black Diaspora.

78 The death of this young man who was extremely well liked by everybody who had ever met him at the age of nineteen, inspired Senghor to write a particularly poignant poem with the title 'Elegy for Philippe-Marguilen'.

79 This is what people in Dakar call Senghor's house, which is situated in the Eastern corner of the city. The fence looks a bit like sharks' teeth and the end of its construction coincided with the screening of *Jaws* in Dakar.

80 He died in his sixty third year.

81 This critique is entirely my own. As has been mentioned above, the Senegalese people

welcomed the news of Senghor's election to the Académie Française with great pride. If one were to conduct a survey on this question today, the outcome would very probably be the same. One has to respect this opinion, but also be allowed to express one's own. Our compatriots are clearly in tune with certain highly placed officials who are very involved in the organization of the Senghor centenary celebrations. The latter, who tend to be, and this needs to be stressed, French citizens and proud of it, don't like to hear a Senegalese President being accused of never having renounced his French nationality. They react to this in a strange way, by saying things like, "It really doesn't matter what nationality you are nowadays", "it just shows how open-minded Senghor was", etc. This kind of thing mainly reveals the embarrassment of the speakers. We are yet to come across a European President who prides himself of having the nationality of a European country which is not his own. And particularly a nationality which has a heavy and contentious history related to his country. Something like this would be an absolute scandal. A famous French singer has recently decided to re-adopt his Belgian citizenship and that was regarded as treason.

82 Cheikh Anta Diop, "When Will We Be Able to Talk About an African Renaissance?" ['Quand pourra-t-on parler d'une renaissance africaine?'] *Le Musée vivant,* numéro spécial 36–37th, November 1948, Paris.

83 Ivan Van Sertima, "Death Shall Not Find Us Thinking That We Shall Die." Introduction to *Great African Thinkers,* vol. 1: *Cheikh Anta Diop* (collective), Transaction Books, New Brunswick (USA) and Oxford (UK), 1986.

84 One should note, however, the extensive *coverage* of the Cairo Symposium by the national daily *Le Soleil,* which, according to its former head Bara Diouf, had been especially stipulated by Senghor himself so that "Cheikh Anta is not left to his own devices in Egypt."

85 Aimé Césaire, *Discourse on Colonialism,* op. cit.

86 Louis Althusser.

87 A second amount of 67 million was granted to Morocco by the European Union on August 23, 2006. According to the Associated Press, " the funds are destined for the emergency programme presented by the Moroccan government to improve the management of the migratory flows and to reinforce the battle against the immigration of illegal stowaways."

88 In fact, the possibility of gaining access to the Schengen area in such a shaky little boat proves indirectly that Africa and Europe are *next-door neighbours* and that what happens at their borders is simply a neighbourhood quarrel which doesn't say its name.

89 Reference to a text message – intended for the humourist Dieudonné after a very controversial sketch – created by the producers of "One cannot please the whole world" (France 3) and broadcast as part of the programme of December 5, 2003: "Would it make you laugh if we produced sketches about the smell of the Blacks?" On September 29, 2005, Marc-Olivier Fogiel and those responsible for the programme and Marc Tessier (at the time president of France Télévisions) were convicted of "racial abuse" in the Montpellier magistrates' court.

90 International Organization of Francophony (*Organisation Internationale de la Francophonie)*

91 Movement of the Democratic Forces of Casamance *(Movement des forces démocratiques de Casamance)*

92 One must remember, though, that the language question has always been central to the anti-apartheid struggle. The rejection of the Afrikaans language was the root cause of the riots that was started by Soweto schoolchildren during the seventies.

93 One even wonders whether one should be surprised by the revisionist naïveté one encounters these days in a country where on February 23, 2005, a law on the positive

aspects of colonialism was implemented. It is frequently forgotten that only paragraph 2 of article 4 of this law was repealed. According to a survey in the *Le Figaro*, this law, which is unique in the world, meets with the approval of 65% of the French population…

94 Mongo Beti, *Lettre ouverte aux Camerounais, ou la deuxième mort de Ruben Um Nyobé,* Peuples Noirs, 1986.

95 Mongo Beti, *La France contre l'Afrique, retour au Cameroun,* La Découverte, 1993; reedited in 2006 with a preface and an epilogue by Odile Tobner.

96 Xavier-François Verschave, *Noir Silence,* Les Arènes, 2000.

97 In Jean-Pierre Warnier, *The Globalization of Culture,* [La Mondialisation de la culture], «Repères», La Découverte, 1999.

98 To this, one can now add the Brazilian and Mexican *telenovelas* which have become such a phenomenon in those countries in the last four or five years.

99 Nationalist State ideology, founded by Kim Il-Sung.

Bibliography

Ayad, Christophe. "Un témoin rwandais récuse le juge Bruguière." *Libération*, December 4, 2006.

Ba, Medhi. *Rwanda, un génocide français*. Paris: L'esprit frappeur, 2000.

Bancel, Nicolas. "Les médias français face au Rwanda. (De l'intervention française de 1990 au génocide)" *Africultures*. January 2002: 30.

Beti, Mongo. *Lettre ouverte aux Camerounais, ou la deuxième mort de Ruben Um Nyobé*. Yaoudé: Peuples Noirs, 1986.

Beti, Mongo. *La France contre l'Afrique, retour au Cameroun*. Paris: La Découverte, 2006.

Braeckmann, Colette. *Les nouveaux prédateurs*. Paris: Fayard, 2003.

Césaire, Aimé. *Discourse on coloniolism*. (Translated by Joan Pinkham) New York: Monthly Review Press, 2001.

Chrétien, Jean-Pierre. *Rwanda, les médias du génocide*. Paris: Karthala, 2000.

Coret, Laure, and François-Xavier Verschave. *L'Horreur qui nous prend au visage. L'État français et le génocide au Rwanda*. Paris: Karthala, 2005.

Dallaire, Roméo. *Shake Hands with the Devil: The Failure of Humanity in Rwanda*. London: Arrow, 2005.

Debré, Bernard. *Le Retour de Mwami, la varie histoire des génocides rwandais*. Paris: Ramsay, 1998.

Diop, Boubacar Boris. *Le Cavalier et son ombre*. Paris: Stock, 1997.

Diop, Boubacar Boris. *Murambi, The Book of Bones*. (Translated by Fiona McLaughlin) Bloomington, IN: Indiana University Press, 2006.

Diop, Cheikh Anta. "Quand pourra-t-on parler d'une renaissance africaine?" Paris: *Le Musée vivant*, November 1948, 36–37.

Diop, Cheikh Anta. *Nations nègres et culture*. Paris: Présence africaine, 1954.

Diop, Cheikh Anta. *Les Fondements économiques et culturels d'un futur État fédéral d'Afrique noire*. Paris: Présence africaine, 1960.

Diop, Cheikh Anta. "Entretien avec Bara Diouf." *La Vie africaine*. March–April 1960, 6.

Diop, Cheikh Anta. "L'art de la contrefaçon." *Taxaw*. Dakar: March 1979.

Diop, Cheikh Mbacké. *Cheikh Anta Diop, l'homme et l'œuvre*. Paris : Présence africaine, 2003.

Djedanoum, Nocky. *Nyamirambo*. Bamako-Lille: Le Figuier/Fest'Africa, 2000.

Gourevitch, Philip. *We Wish to Inform You that Tomorrow We Will Be Killed with Our Families:*

Stories From Rwanda. New York: Farrar, Straus and Giroux, 1999.
Gouteux, Jean-Paul. *La Nuit rwandaise. L'implication française dans le dernier génocide du siècle.* Paris: Dagorno, 2004.
Guland, Olivier. *Le Pen, Mégret et les Juifs.* Paris: La Découverte, 2000.
Ilboudo, Monique. *Murekatete.* Bamako-Lille: Le Figuier/Fest'Africa, 2000.
Kayimahe, Venuste. *France-Rwanda: les coulisses du génocide.* Paris: L'esprit frappeur/Dagorno, 2003.
Kayitesi, Annick. *Nous existons encore.* Paris: Michel Lafon, 2004.
Lambo, Koulsy. *La Phalène des collines.* Paris: Le Serpent à Plumes, 2000.
Mandela, Nelson. *Long Walk to Freedom.* New York: Little, Brown & Co, 1995.
Monenembo, Tierno. *The Oldest Orphan.* Lincoln, Nebraska: Bison Books, 2004.
Mukagasana, Yolande. *La Mort ne veut pas de moi.* Paris: Fixot, 1997.
Mukagasana, Yolande. *N'aie pas peur de savoir.* Paris: Robert Laffont, 1999; J'ai Lu, 2000.
Mukagasana, Yolande. *Les Blessures du silence.* Paris: Actes Sud, 2001.
Mukamuganga, Madeleine. *Rwanda, du bonheur à l'horreur, j'y étais.* Neuilly Plaisance, France: Cultures Croisées, 2005.
Muyawayo, Esther, and Souâd Belhaddad. *Survivantes.* Paris: Éditions de l'Aube, 2004.
Muyawayo, Esther, and Souâd Belhaddad. *La Fleur de Stéphanie, le Rwanda entre réconciliation et déni.* Paris: Flammarion, 2006.
Mwangi, Meja. *Great Sadness.* (unpublished)
Orsenna, Erik. "J'ai honte!" *Le Monde,* January 5, 2002
Prunier, Gérard. *Rwanda, 1959–1996 – histoire d'un génocide.* Paris: Dagorno, 1997.
Prunier, Gérard. *Rwanda: le génocide.* Paris: Dagorno, 1998.
Rémy, Jean-Philippe. "Les erreurs et les étranges témoins du juge Bruguière." *Le Monde,* November 28, 2006.
Rurangwa, Révérien. *Génocidés.* Paris: Presses de la Renaissance, 2006.
Saint-Exupéry, Patrick de, *L'Inavouable: la France au Rwanda.* Paris: Les Arènes, 2004.
Sehene, Benjamin. *Le piège ethnique.* Paris: Dagorno, 1999.
Sehene, Benjamin. *Le feu sous la soutane.* Paris: L'esprit frappeur, 2005.
Tadjo, Véronique & Véronique Wakerley. *The Shadow of Imana: Travels in the Heart of Rwanda.* London: Heinemann, 2002.
Umutesi, Chantal. *La Paix dans l'âme.* Paris: Klanba Éditions, 2004.
Van Sertima, Ivan. "Death Shall Not Find Us Thinking That We Shall Die." Introduction to *Great African Thinkers,* vol. 1*: Cheikh Anta Diop.* New Brunswick-Oxford: Transaction Books, 1986.
Verschave, François-Xavier. *Complicité de génocide? La politique de la France au Rwanda.* Paris: La Découverte, 1994.
Verschave, François-Xavier. *Noir Silence.* Paris: Les Arènes, 2000.
Vianney Ruranga. Jean-Marie. *Le Génocide des Tutsi expliqué à un étranger.* Bamako-Lille: Le Figuier/Fest'Africa, 2001.
Vianney Ruranga. *Un Rwandais sur les routes de l'exil.* Paris: L'Harmattan, 2005.
Vianney Ruranga. *Au sortir de l'enfer.* Paris: l'Harmattan, 2007.
Waberi, Abdourahman. *Moisson de crânes.* Paris: Le Serpent à Plumes, 2000.
Warnier, Jean-Pierre. "Repères." *La Mondialisation de la culture.* Paris: La Découverte, 1999.

Collective/Group Publications

"Les Relations évolutionnaires des groupes humains à partir d'une analyse des polymorphismes de l'AND nucléaire." Nature. *London*: February 1986, 6: 319.
Aucun témoin ne doit survivre. (collectif) Paris: Karthala, 1999.
Death, Despair, Defiance. London: African Rights, 1994.
Rwanda, the Preventable Genocide. Organization of African Unity. 2000.

Index